Elizabeth Ward

LEVEL—EASY

Arrangements of 10 Christmas Favorites for

Volume 5

INSTRUMENTAL HYMN SOLOS

C treble, C bass, B♭, F, E♭, and Alto clef instruments

Three Accompaniment Options:
- Keyboard
- CD trax
- MIDI

The piano folio is only temporarily stapled to the center of this book. It is easily removed by a slight pull outward.

Copyright © 2002 by Lillenas Publishing Company. All rights reserved. Litho in U.S.A.

Lillenas PUBLISHING COMPANY
Kansas City, MO 64141
lillenas.com

The First Noel

W. SANDYS' CHRISTMAS CAROLS

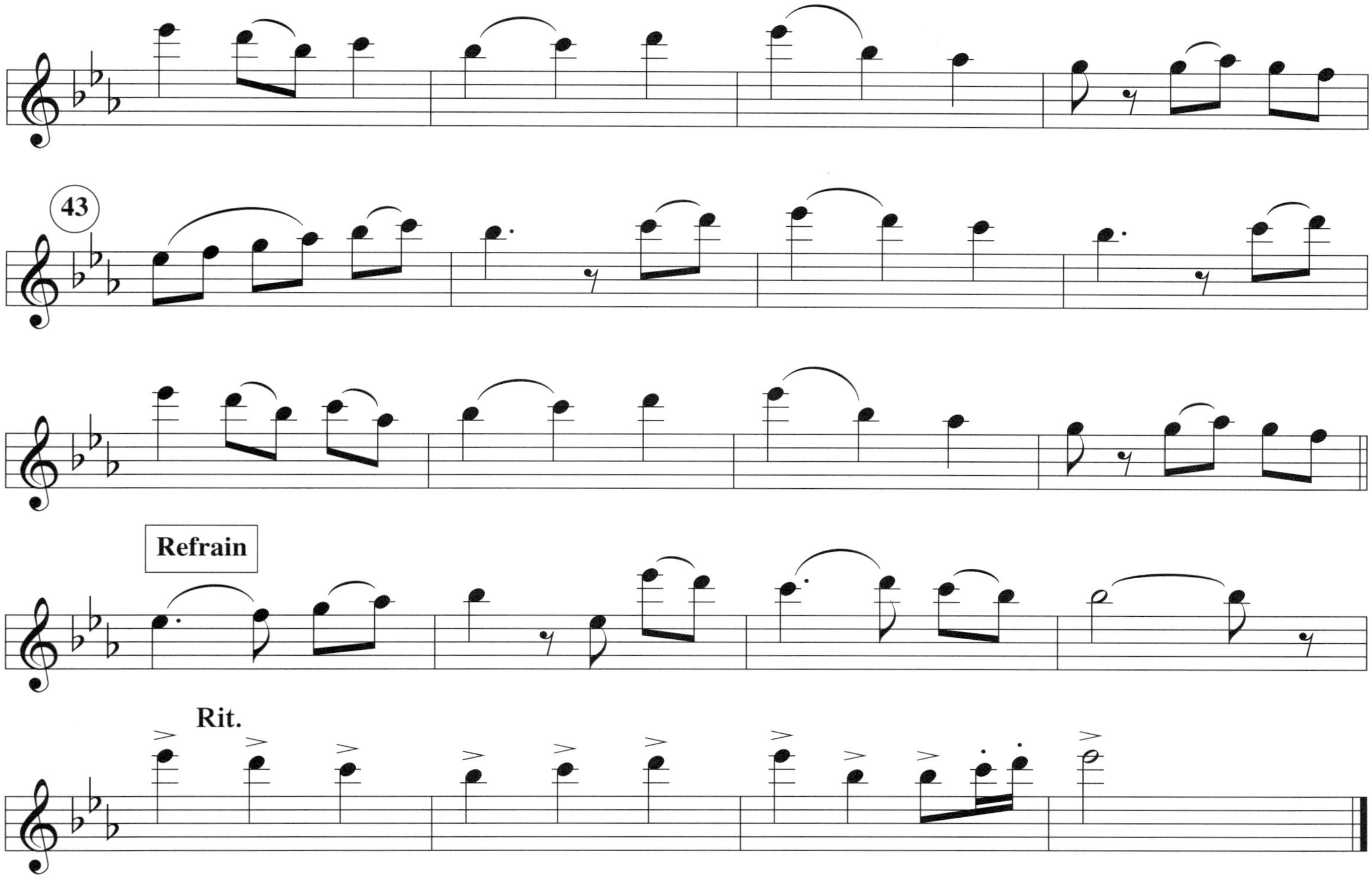

Silent Night! Holy Night!

C Instrument

FRANZ GRUBER

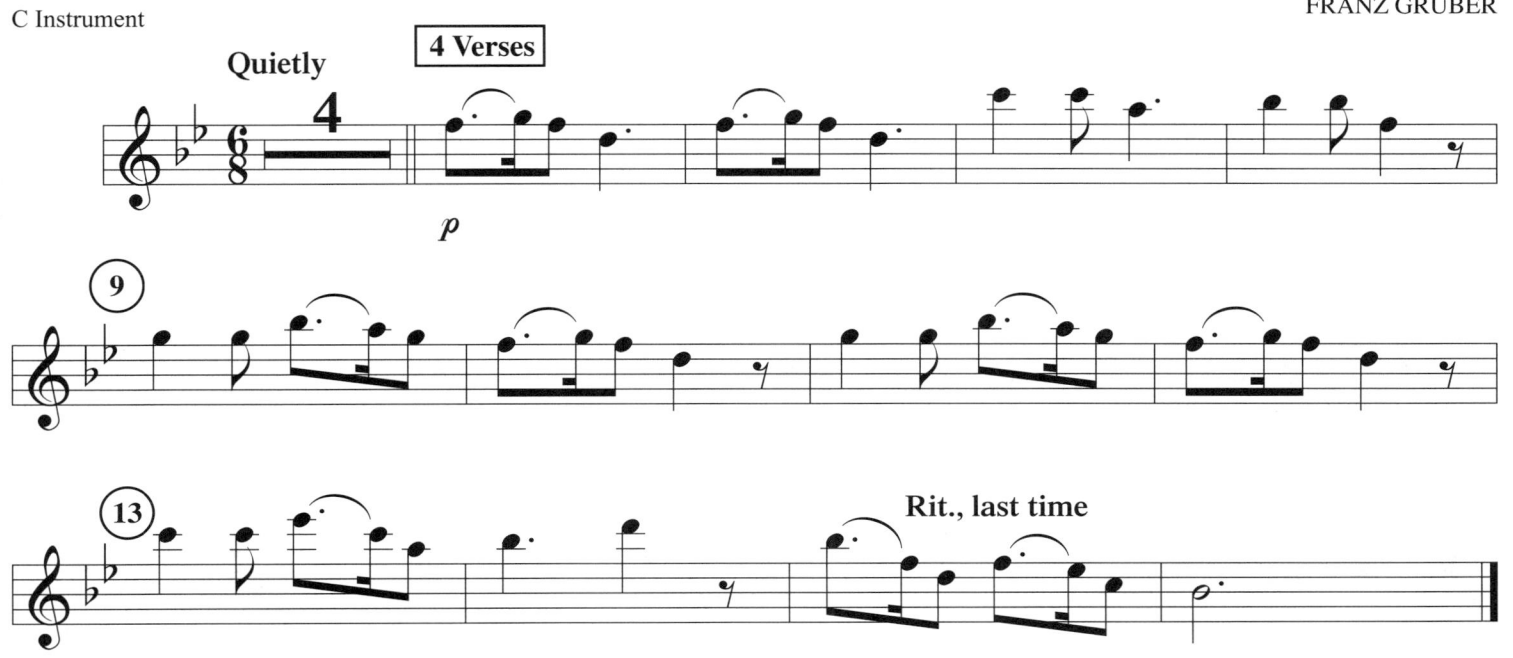

O Come, O Come, Emmanuel

PLAINSONG
adapted by Thomas Helmore

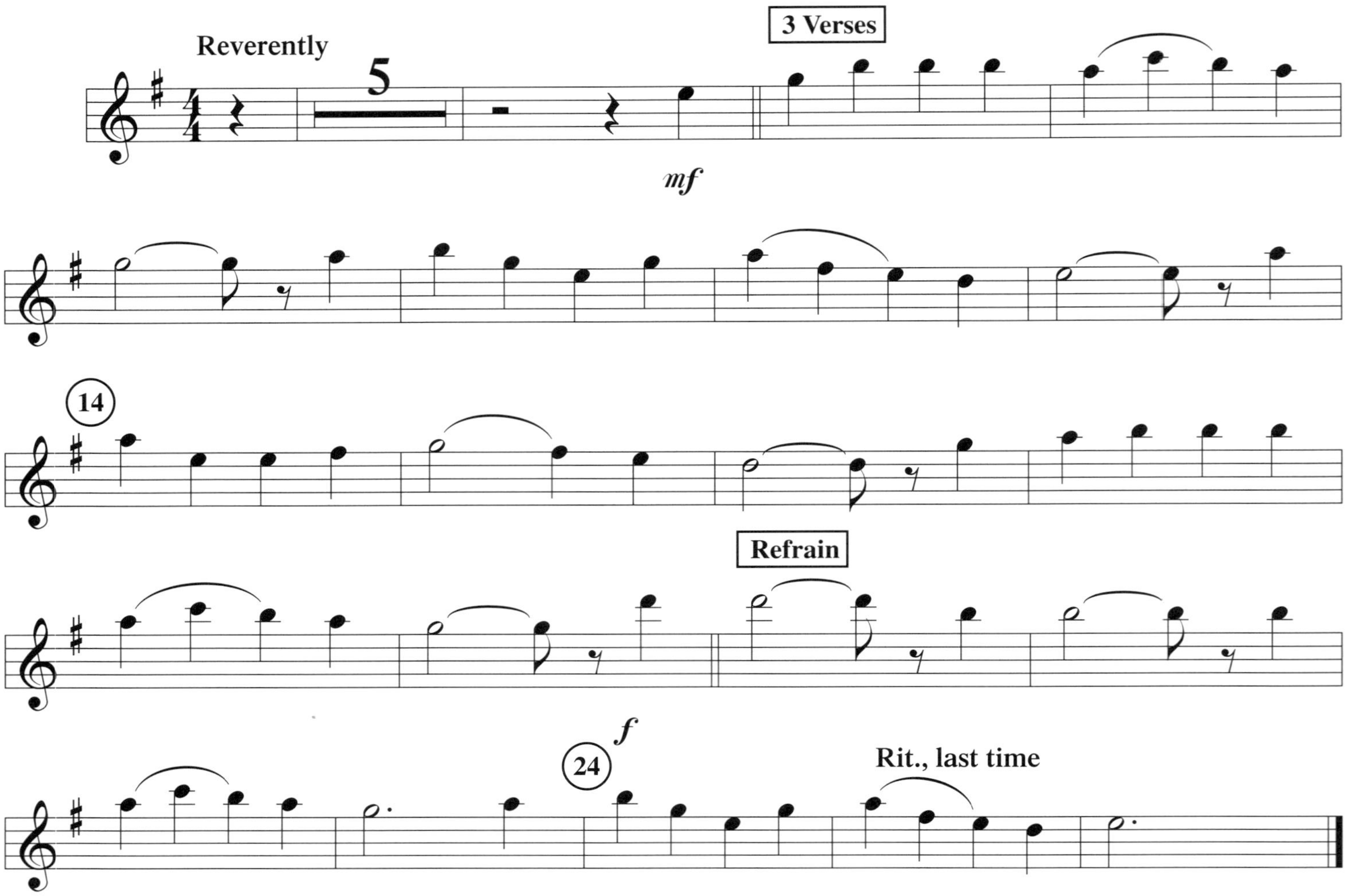

Arr. © 2002 by Lillenas Publishing Company (SESAC). All rights reserved.
Administered by The Copyright Company, 1025 16th Avenue South, Nashville, TN 37212.

O Little Town of Bethlehem

LEWIS H. REDNER

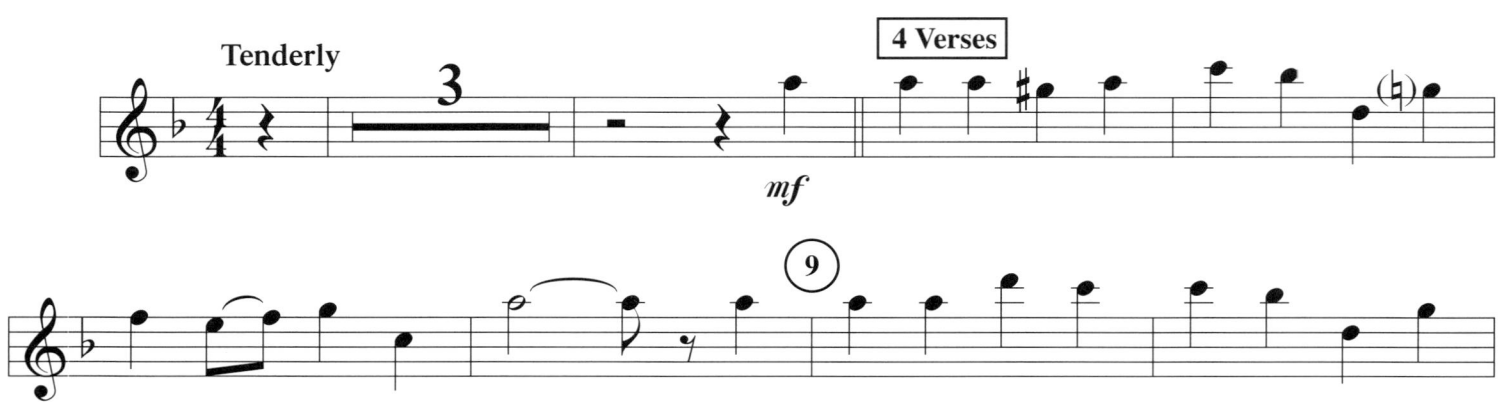

Arr. © 2002 by Lillenas Publishing Company (SESAC). All rights reserved.
Administered by The Copyright Company, 1025 16th Avenue South, Nashville, TN 37212.

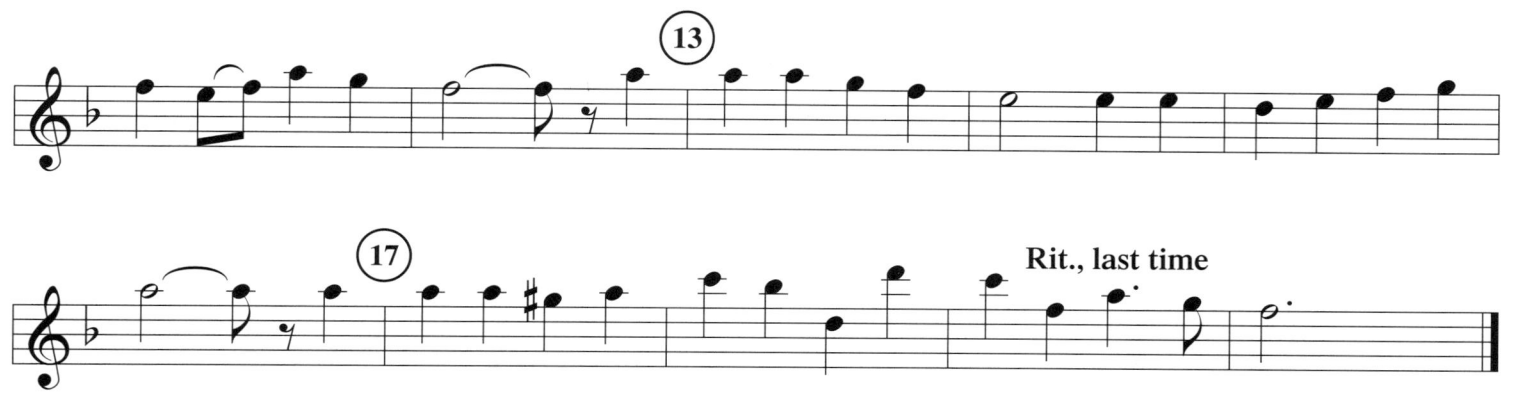

It Came upon the Midnight Clear

C Instrument

RICHARD S. WILLIS

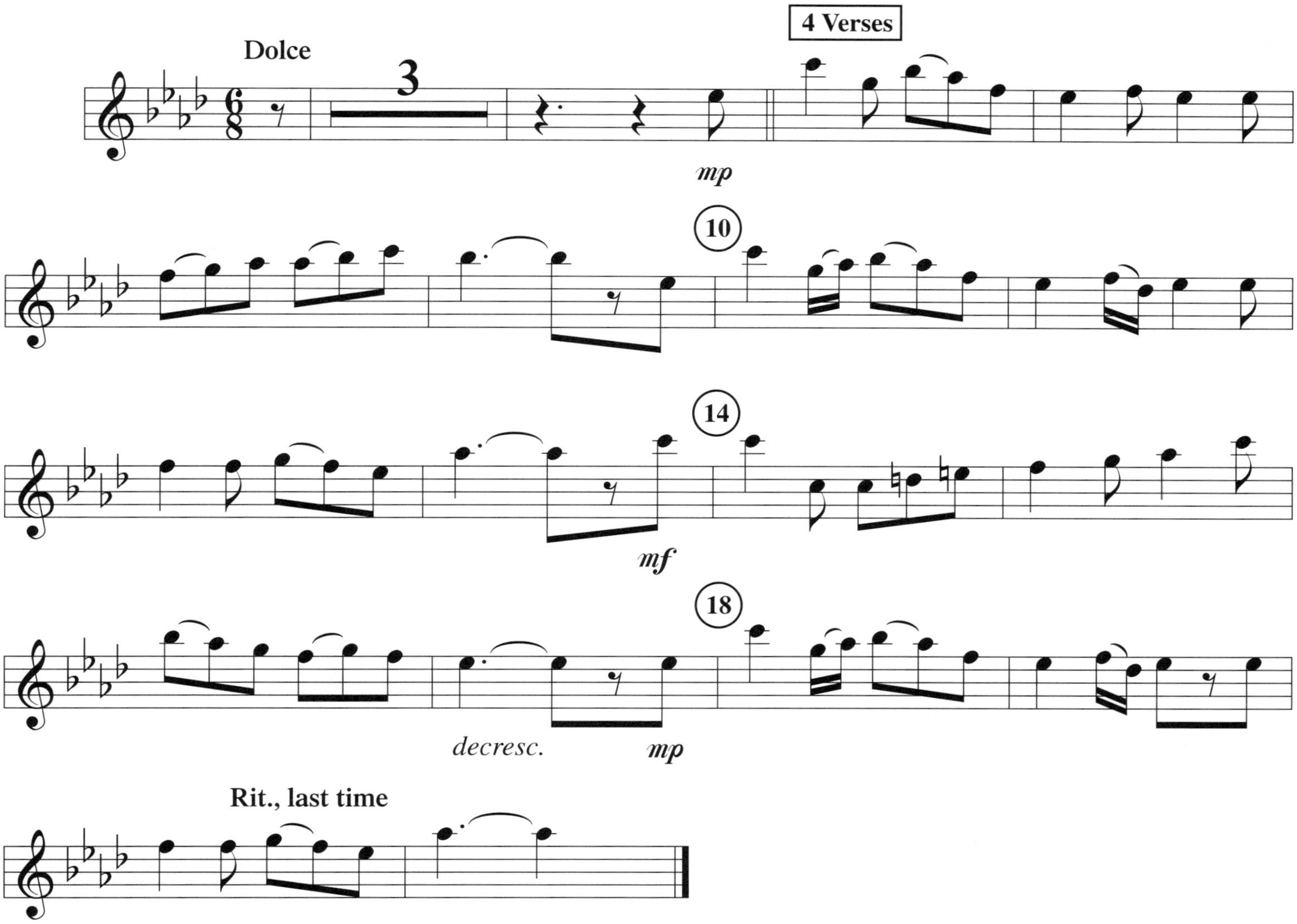

Arr. © 2002 by Lillenas Publishing Company (SESAC). All rights reserved.
Administered by The Copyright Company, 1025 16th Avenue South, Nashville, TN 37212.

Joy to the World

C Instrument

GEORGE FREDERICK HANDEL

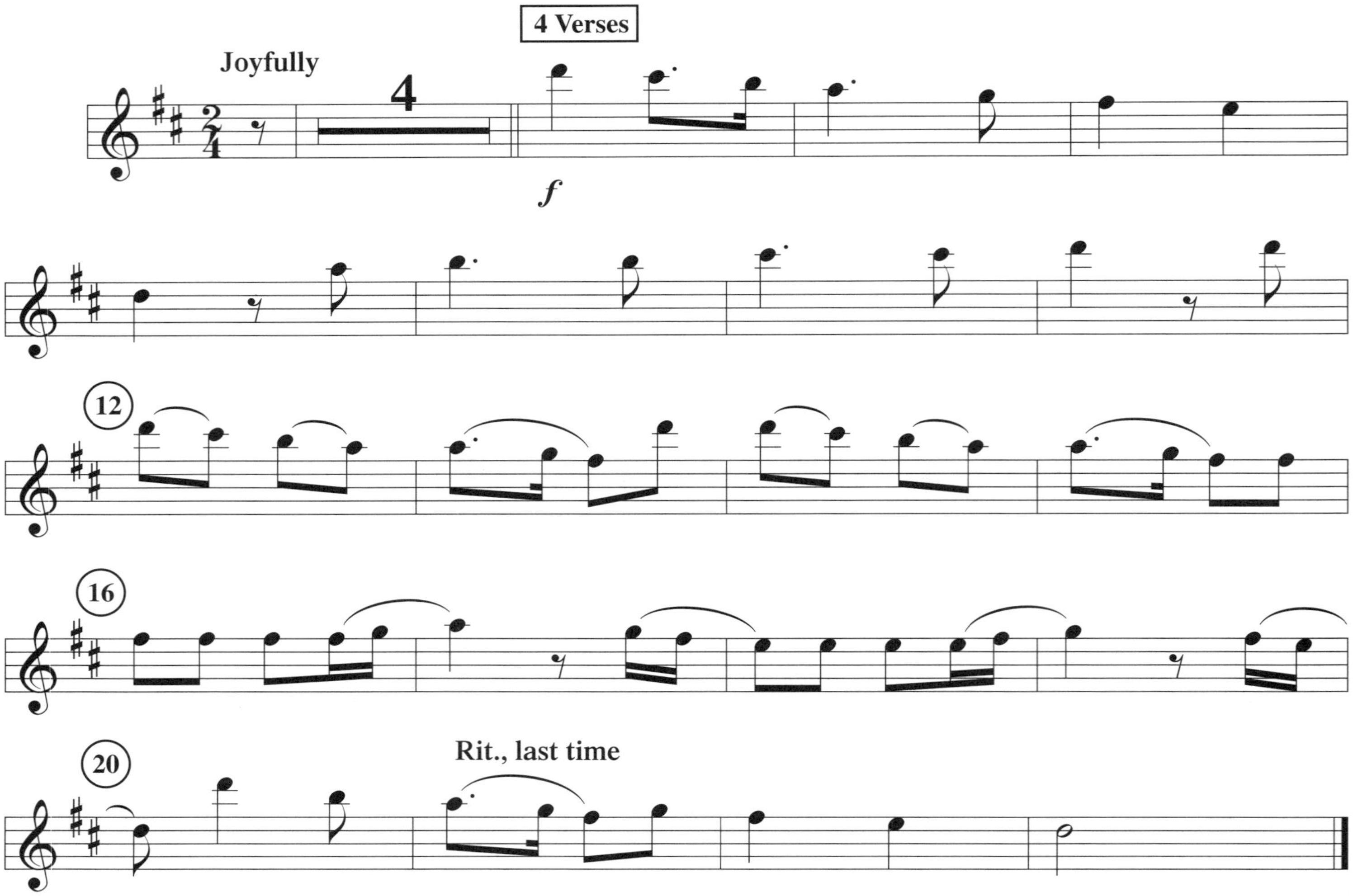

4 Verses
Joyfully
4
f
12
16
20
Rit., last time

O Come, All Ye Faithful

C Instrument

attr. to JOHN F. WADE

Jubilantly
3
3 Verses
mf
9

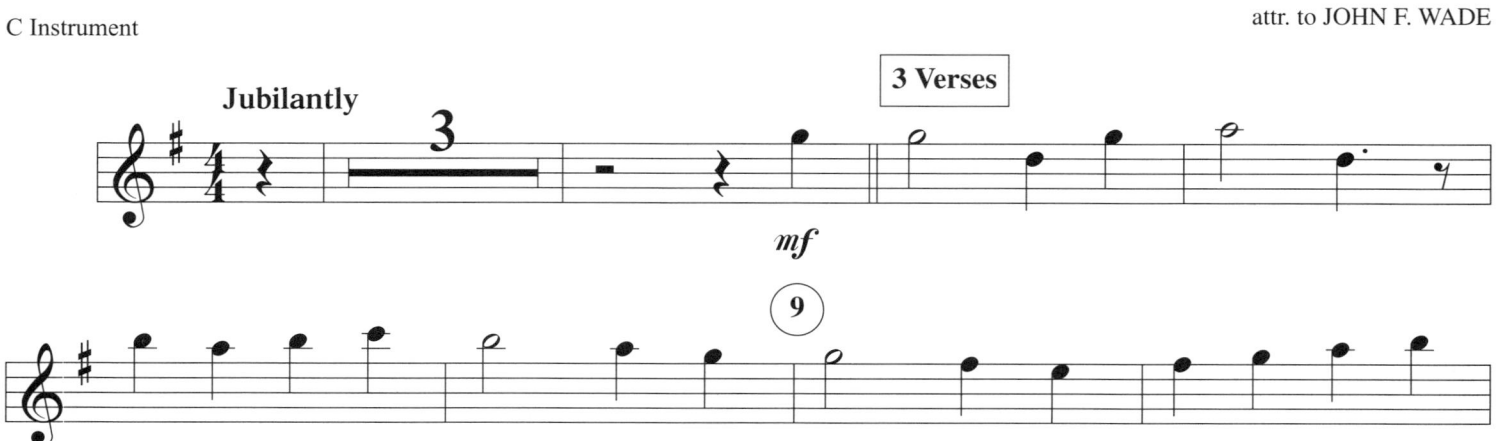

Away in a Manger

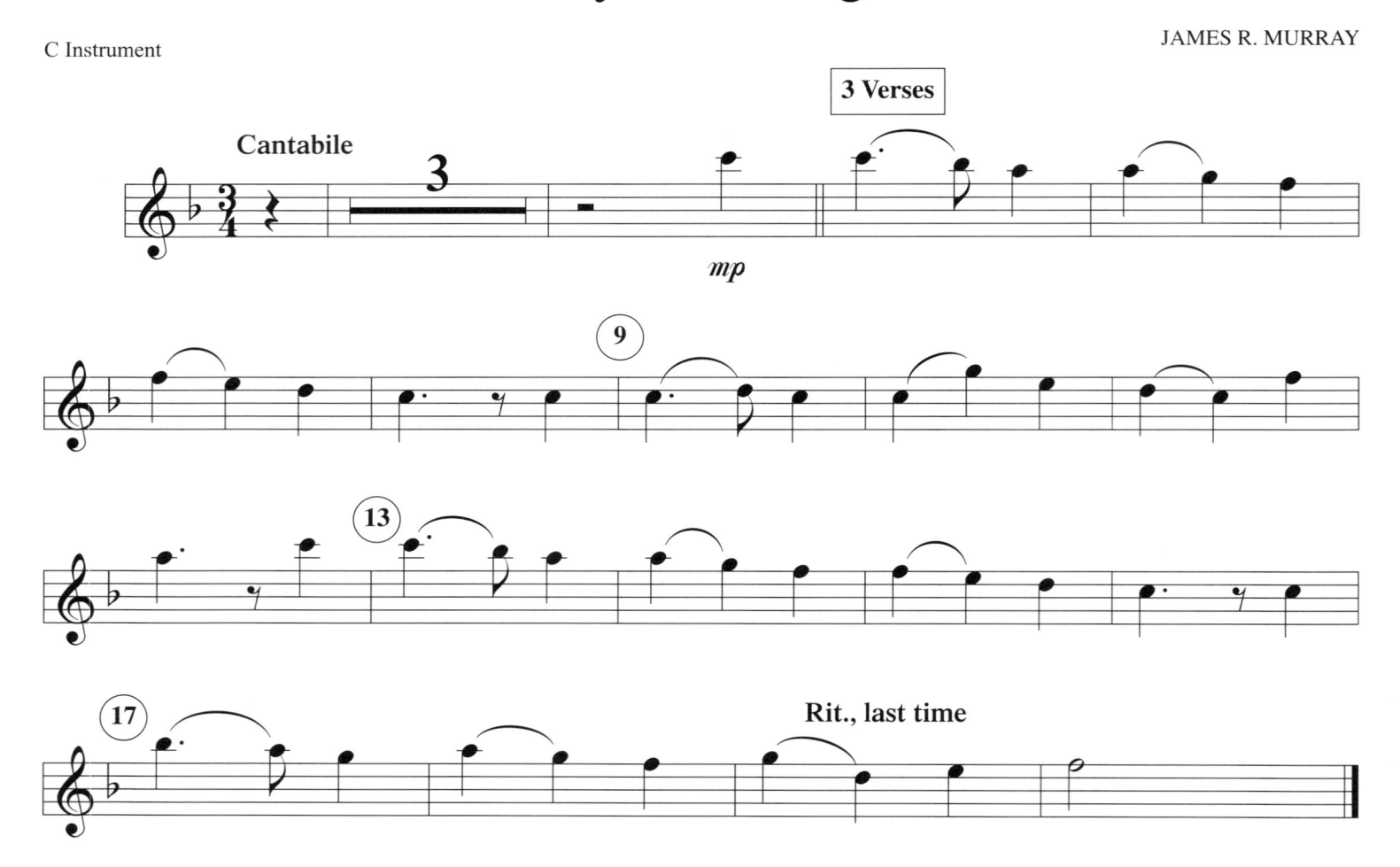

C Instrument

JAMES R. MURRAY

Cantabile / 3 Verses / *mp*

Rit., last time

Arr. © 2002 by Lillenas Publishing Company (SESAC). All rights reserved.
Administered by The Copyright Company, 1025 16th Avenue South, Nashville, TN 37212.

What Child Is This?

C Instrument

TRADITIONAL ENGLISH MELODY

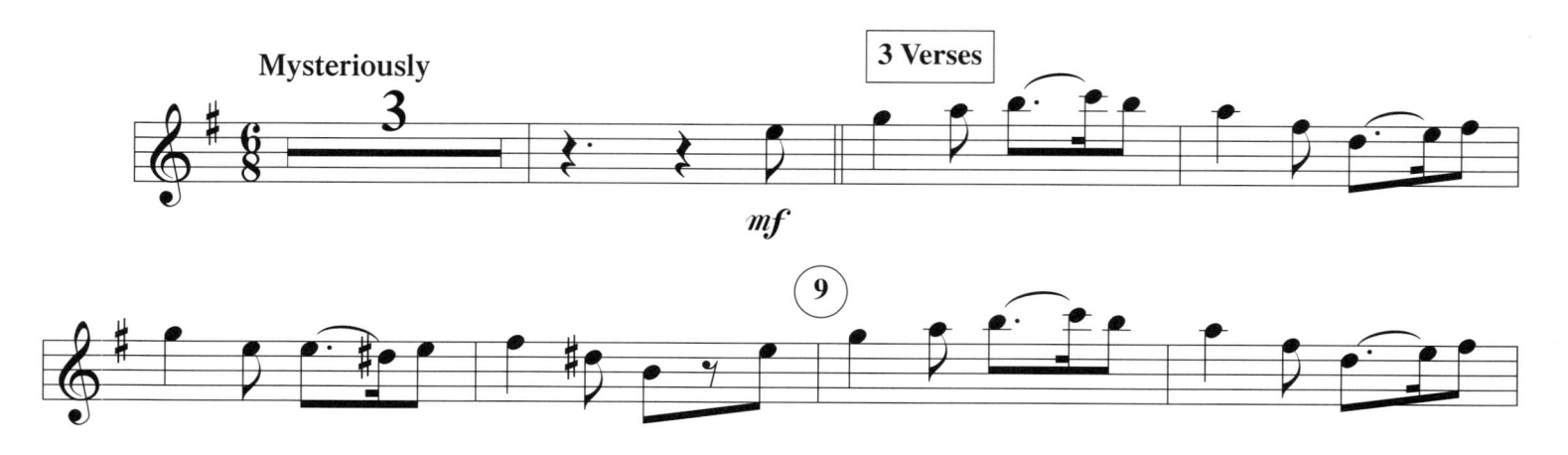

Mysteriously / 3 Verses / *mf*

Arr. © 2002 by Lillenas Publishing Company (SESAC). All rights reserved.
Administered by The Copyright Company, 1025 16th Avenue South, Nashville, TN 37212.

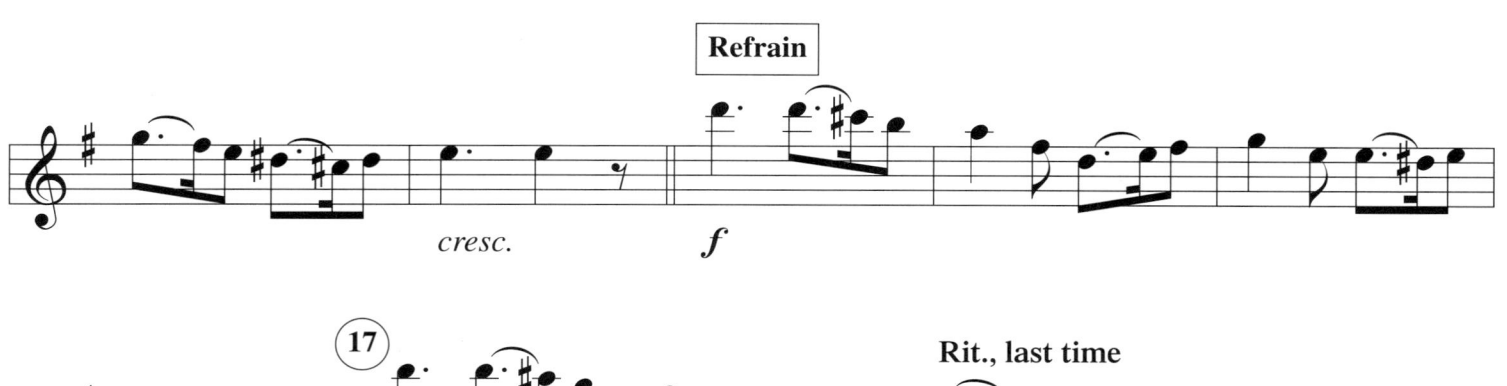

While Shepherds Watched Their Flocks

GEORGE FREDERICK HANDEL

C Instrument

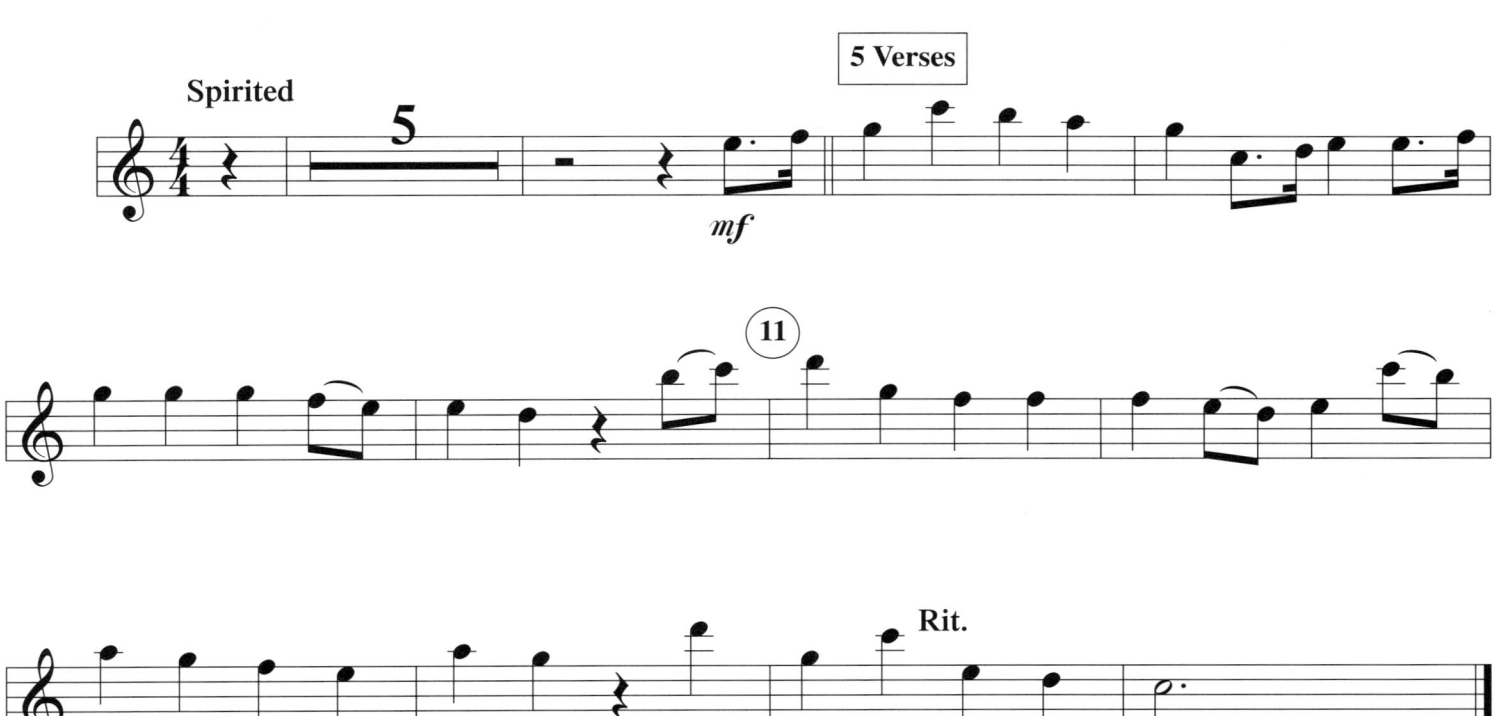

Arr. © 2002 by Lillenas Publishing Company (SESAC). All rights reserved.
Administered by The Copyright Company, 1025 16th Avenue South, Nashville, TN 37212.

The First Noel

C Bass Instrument

W. SANDYS' CHRISTMAS CAROLS

11

Silent Night! Holy Night!

FRANZ GRUBER

C Bass Instrument

Arr. © 2002 by Lillenas Publishing Company (SESAC). All rights reserved.
Administered by The Copyright Company, 1025 16th Avenue South, Nashville, TN 37212.

O Come, O Come, Emmanuel

PLAINSONG
adapted by Thomas Helmore

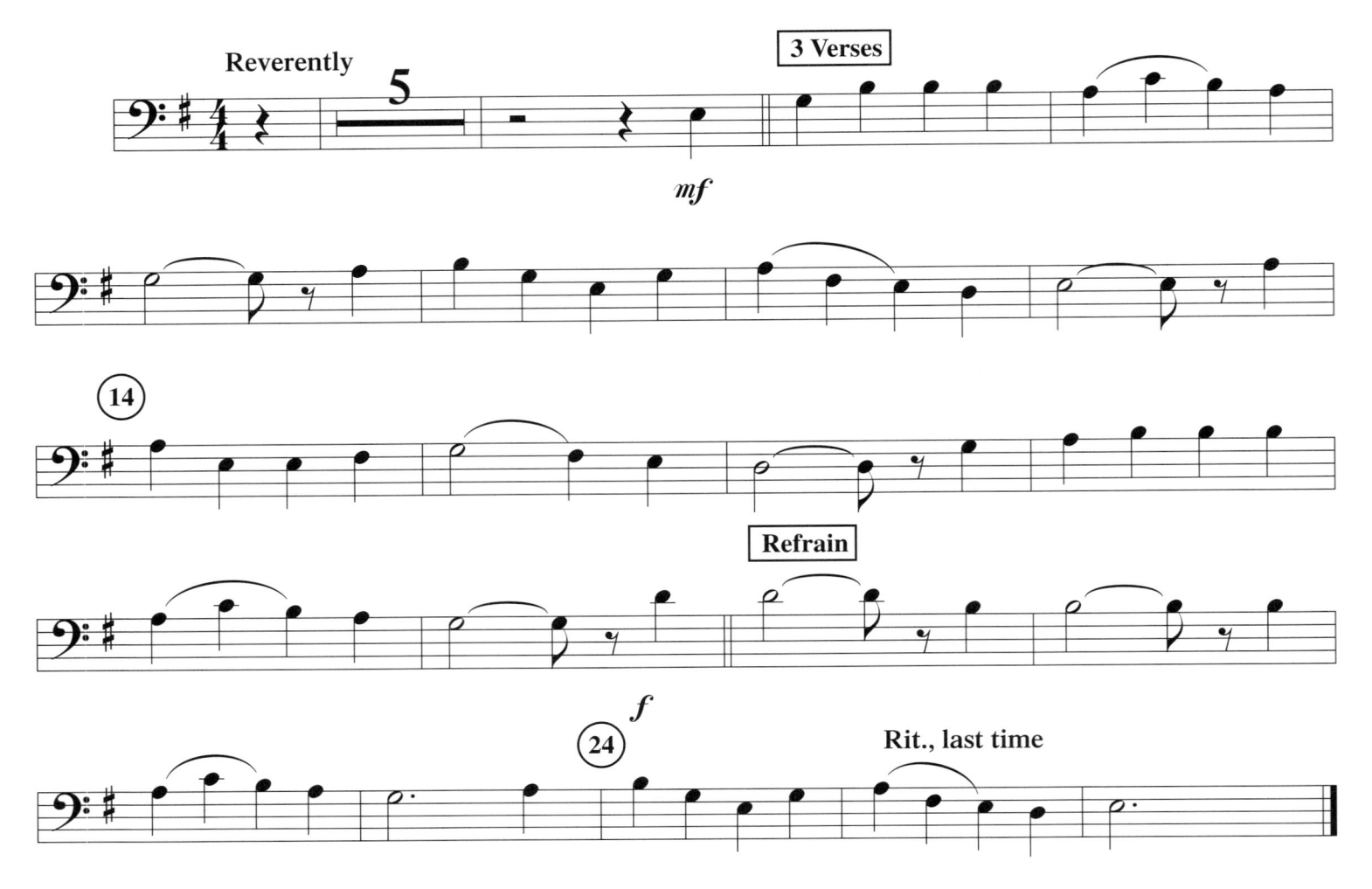

C Bass Instrument

Arr. © 2002 by Lillenas Publishing Company (SESAC). All rights reserved.
Administered by The Copyright Company, 1025 16th Avenue South, Nashville, TN 37212.

O Little Town of Bethlehem

LEWIS H. REDNER

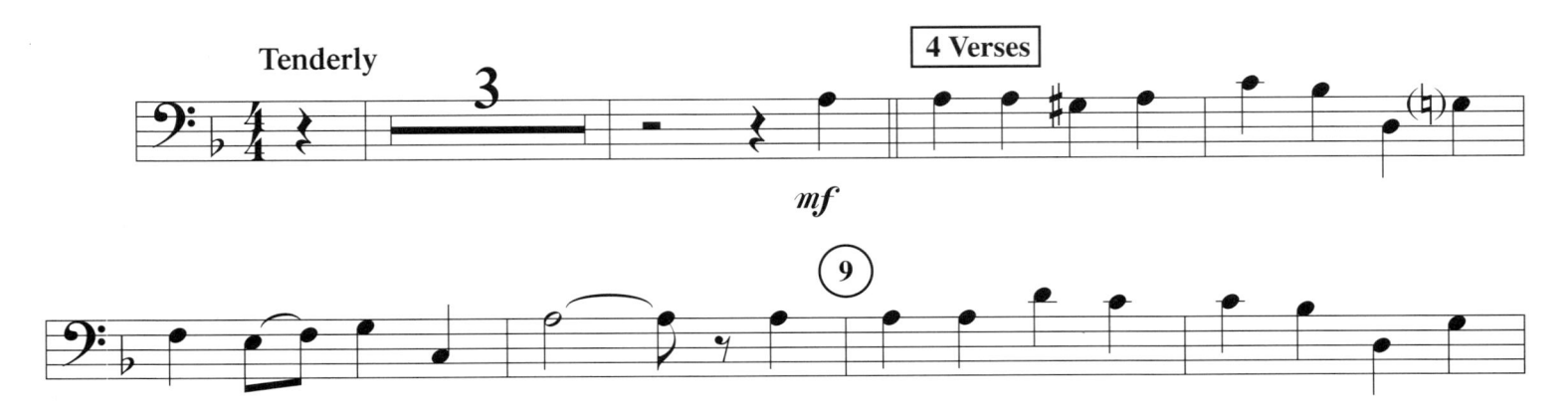

C Bass Instrument

Arr. © 2002 by Lillenas Publishing Company (SESAC). All rights reserved.
Administered by The Copyright Company, 1025 16th Avenue South, Nashville, TN 37212.

13

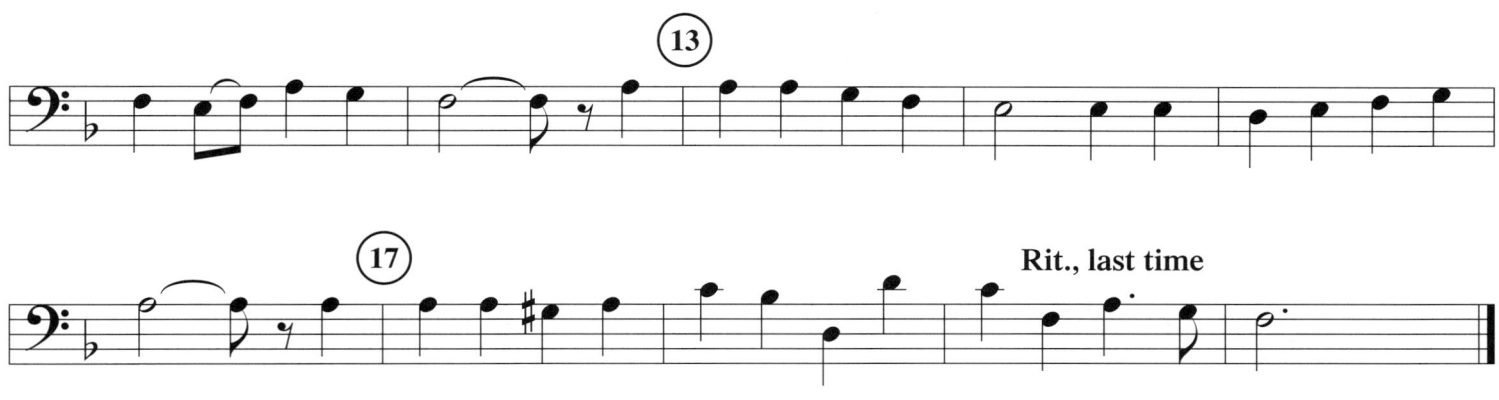

It Came upon the Midnight Clear

RICHARD S. WILLIS

C Bass Instrument

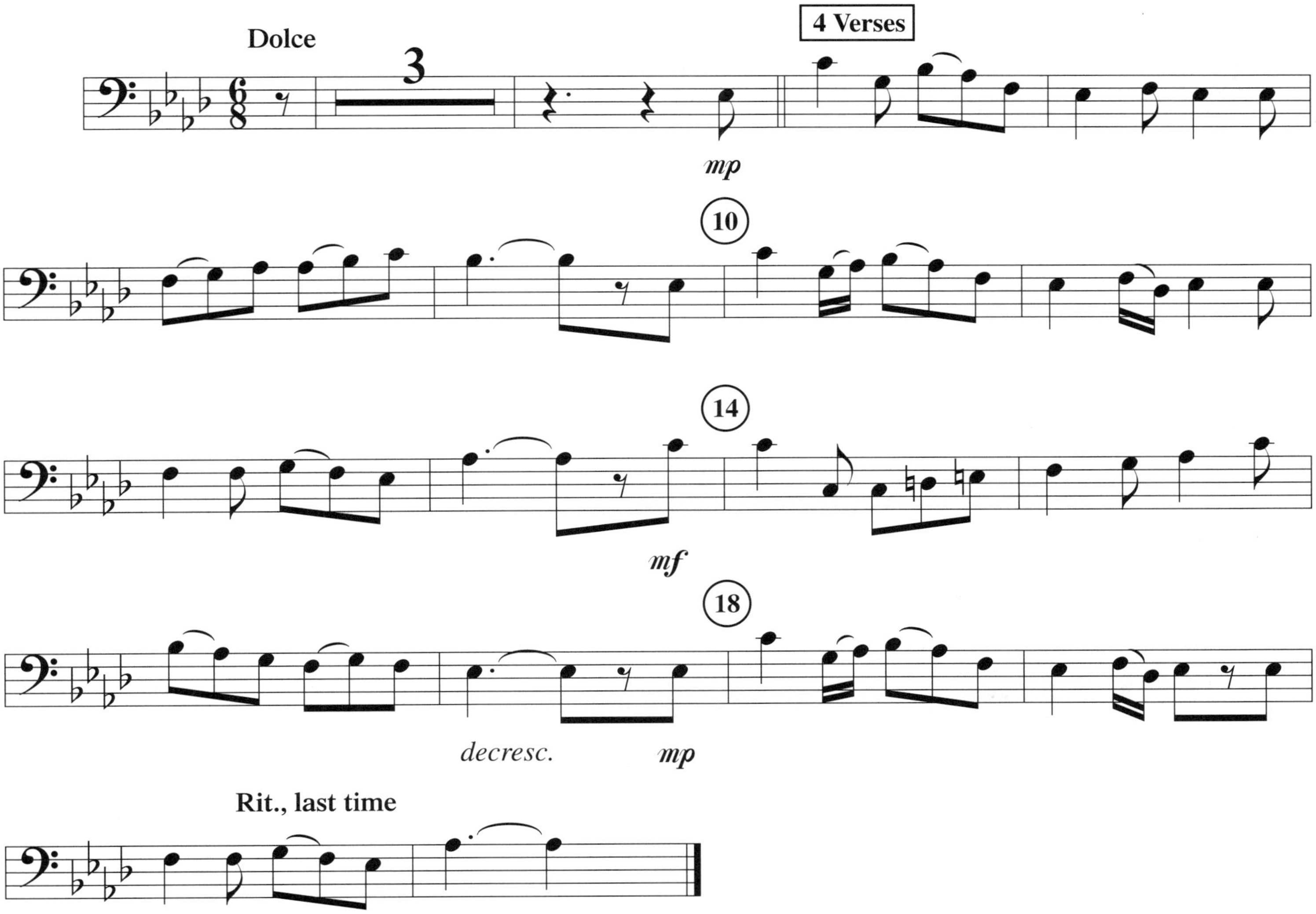

Arr. © 2002 by Lillenas Publishing Company (SESAC). All rights reserved.
Administered by The Copyright Company, 1025 16th Avenue South, Nashville, TN 37212.

Joy to the World

GEORGE FREDERICK HANDEL

C Bass Instrument

O Come, All Ye Faithful

attr. to JOHN F. WADE

C Bass Instrument

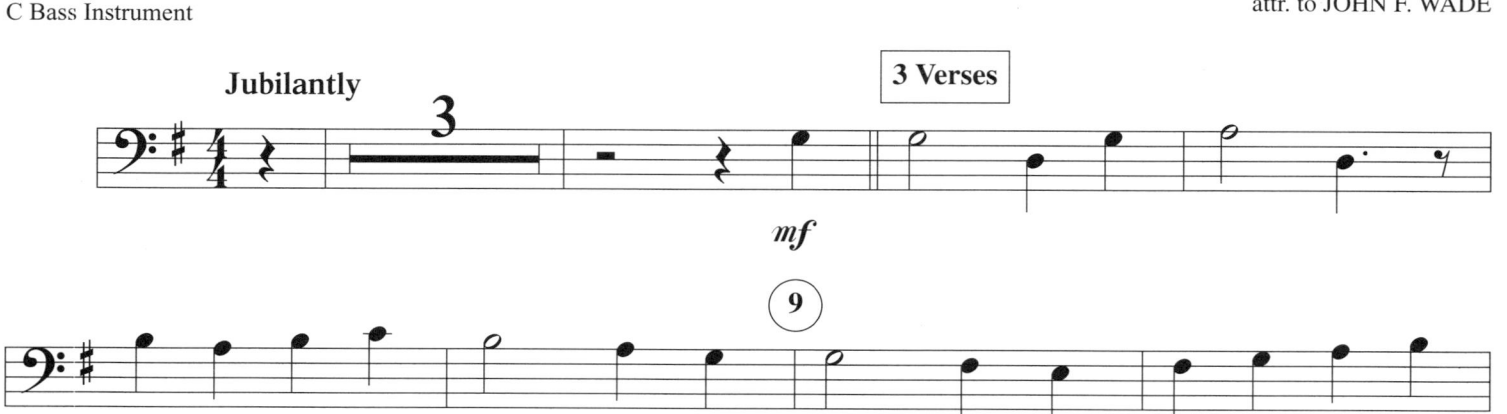

Away in a Manger

C Bass Instrument

JAMES R. MURRAY

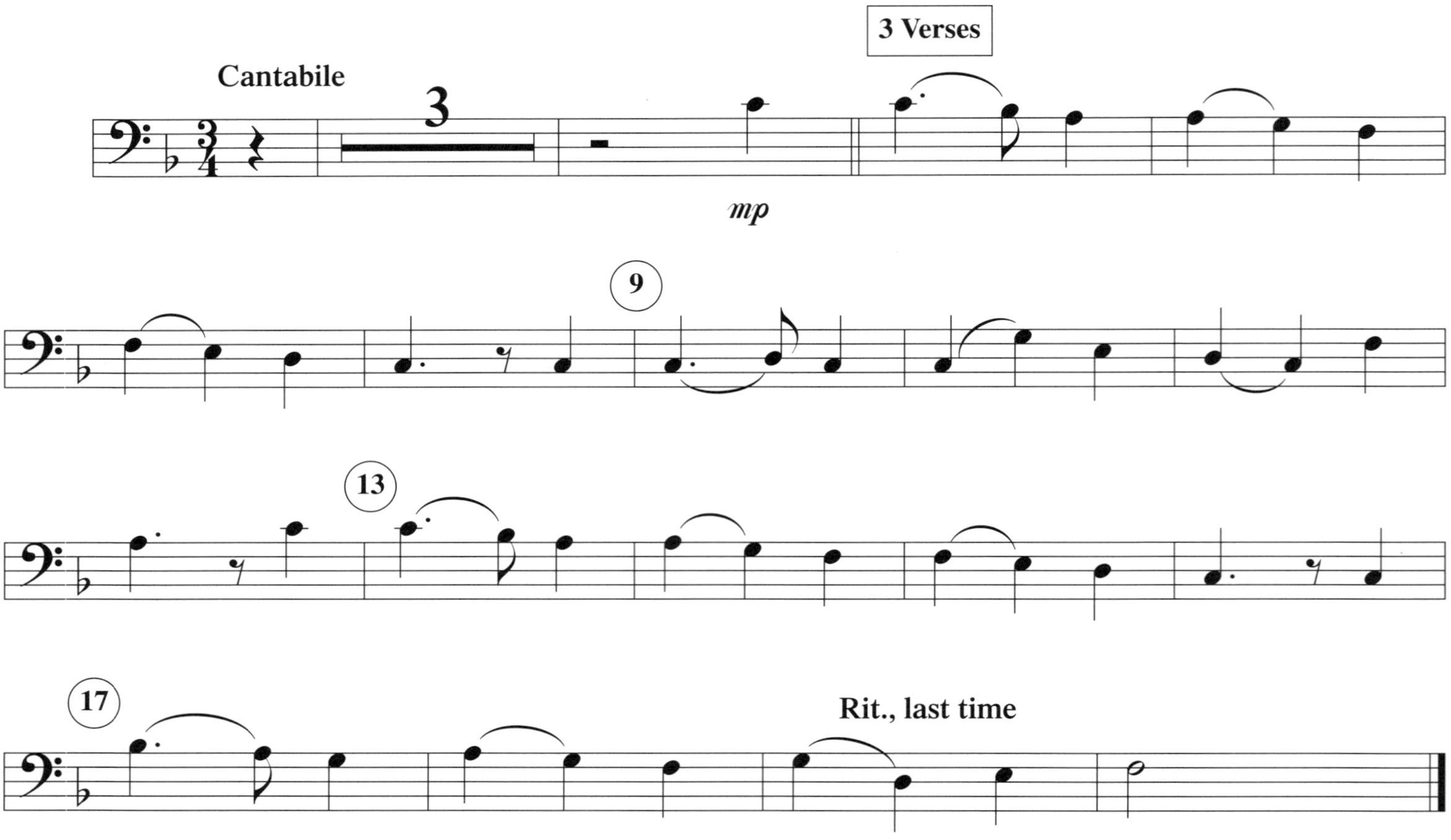

Arr. © 2002 by Lillenas Publishing Company (SESAC). All rights reserved.
Administered by The Copyright Company, 1025 16th Avenue South, Nashville, TN 37212.

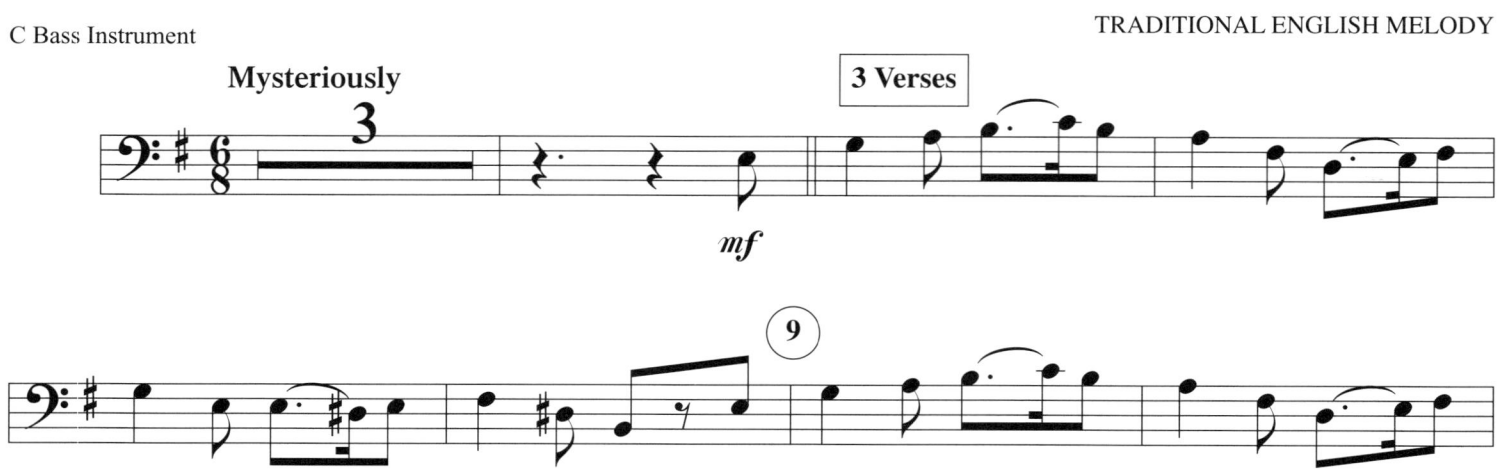

What Child Is This?

C Bass Instrument

TRADITIONAL ENGLISH MELODY

Arr. © 2002 by Lillenas Publishing Company (SESAC). All rights reserved.
Administered by The Copyright Company, 40 Music Square East, Nashville, TN 37203

17

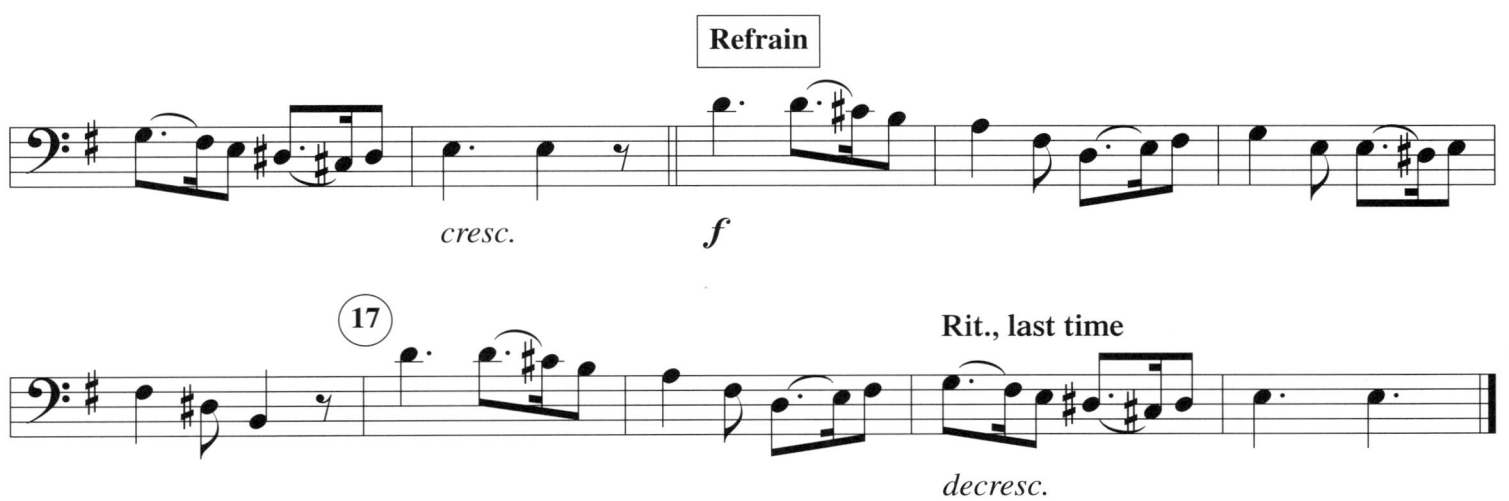

While Shepherds Watched Their Flocks

GEORGE FREDERICK HANDEL

C Bass Instrument

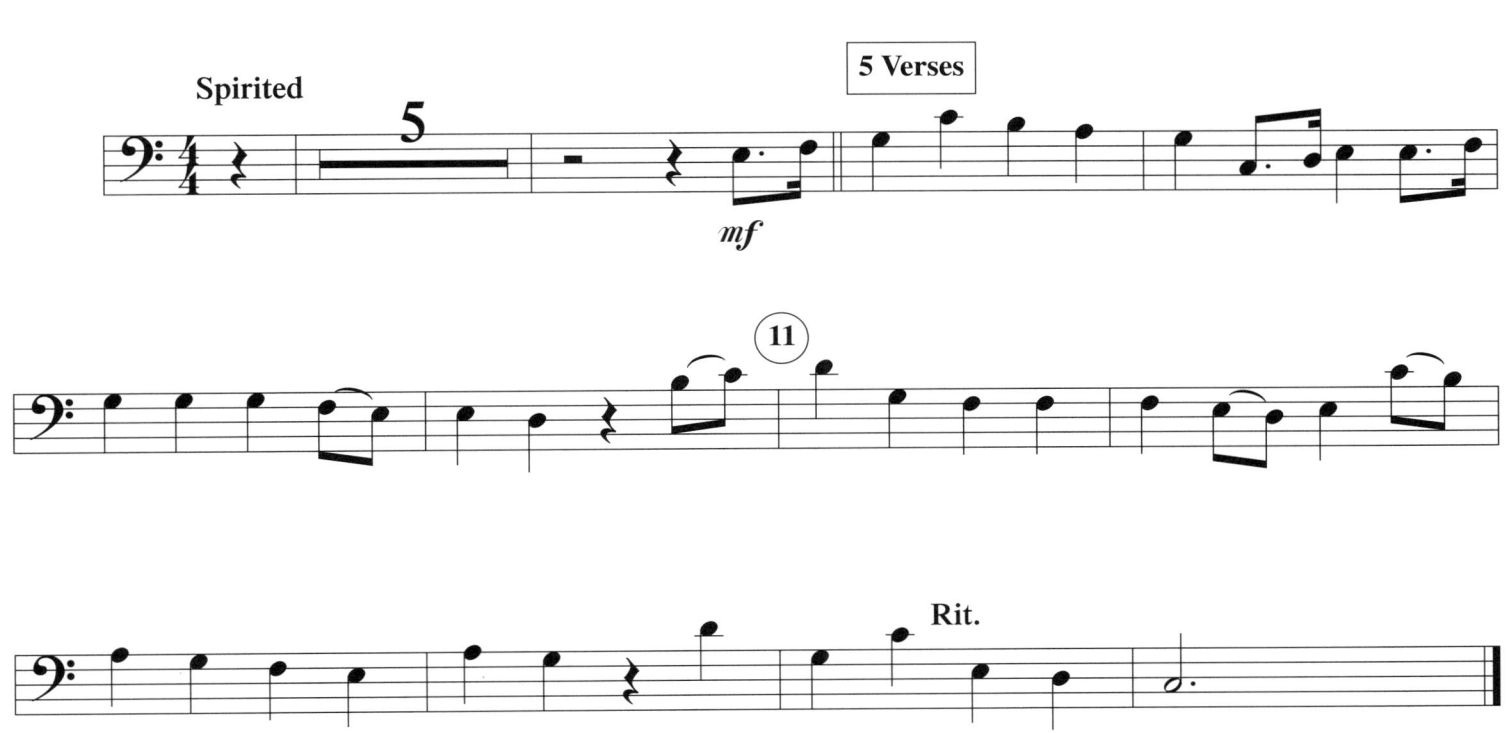

Arr. © 2002 by Lillenas Publishing Company (SESAC). All rights reserved.
Administered by The Copyright Company, 40 Music Square East, Nashville, TN 37203

The First Noel

Bb Instrument

W. SANDYS' CHRISTMAS CAROLS

19

Silent Night! Holy Night!

FRANZ GRUBER

Arr. © 2002 by Lillenas Publishing Company (SESAC). All rights reserved.
Administered by The Copyright Company, 1025 16th Avenue South, Nashville, TN 37212.

O Come, O Come, Emmanuel

Bb Instrument

PLAINSONG
adapted by Thomas Helmore

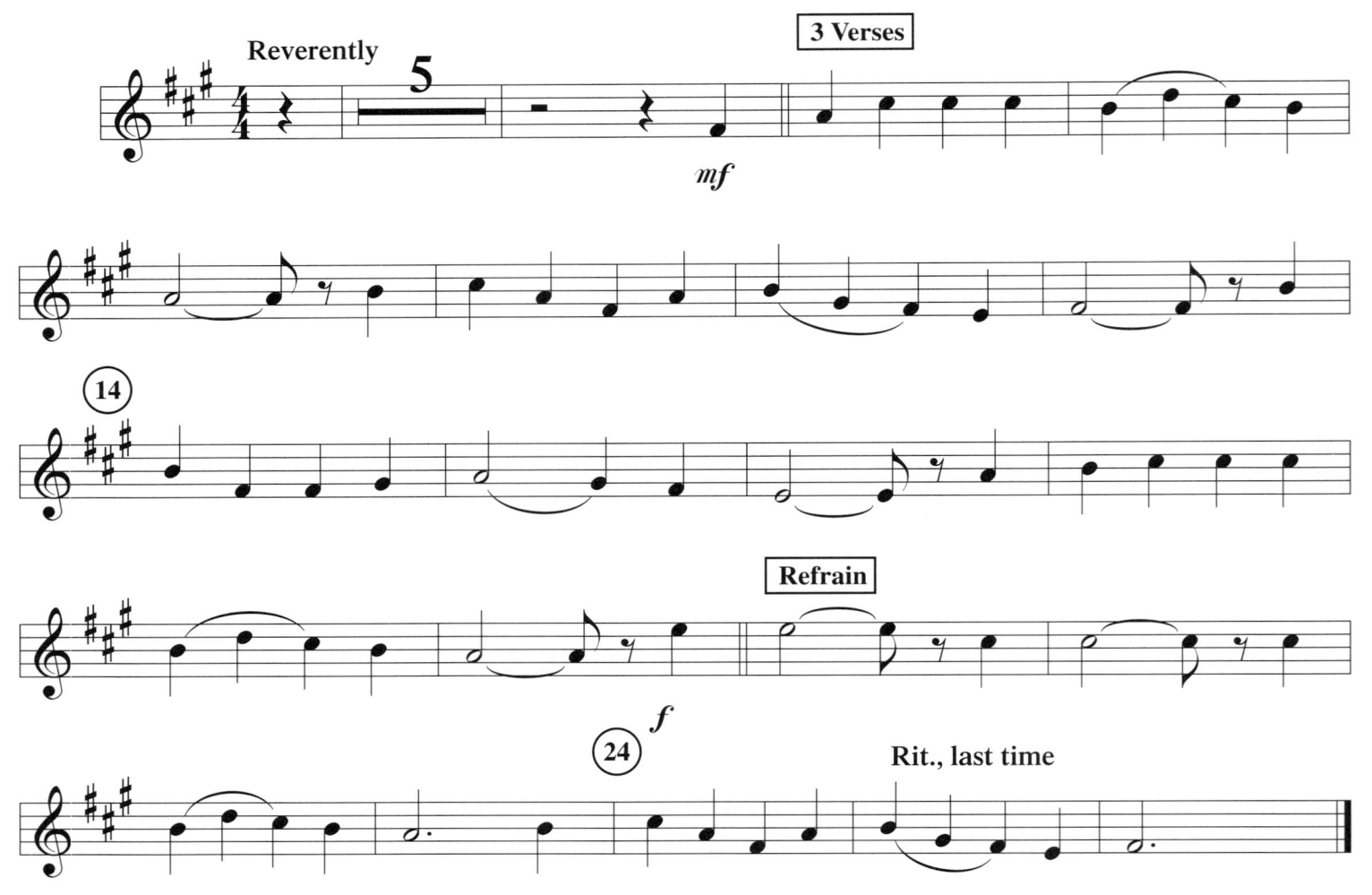

Arr. © 2002 by Lillenas Publishing Company (SESAC). All rights reserved.
Administered by The Copyright Company, 1025 16th Avenue South, Nashville, TN 37212.

O Little Town of Bethlehem

Bb Instrument

LEWIS H. REDNER

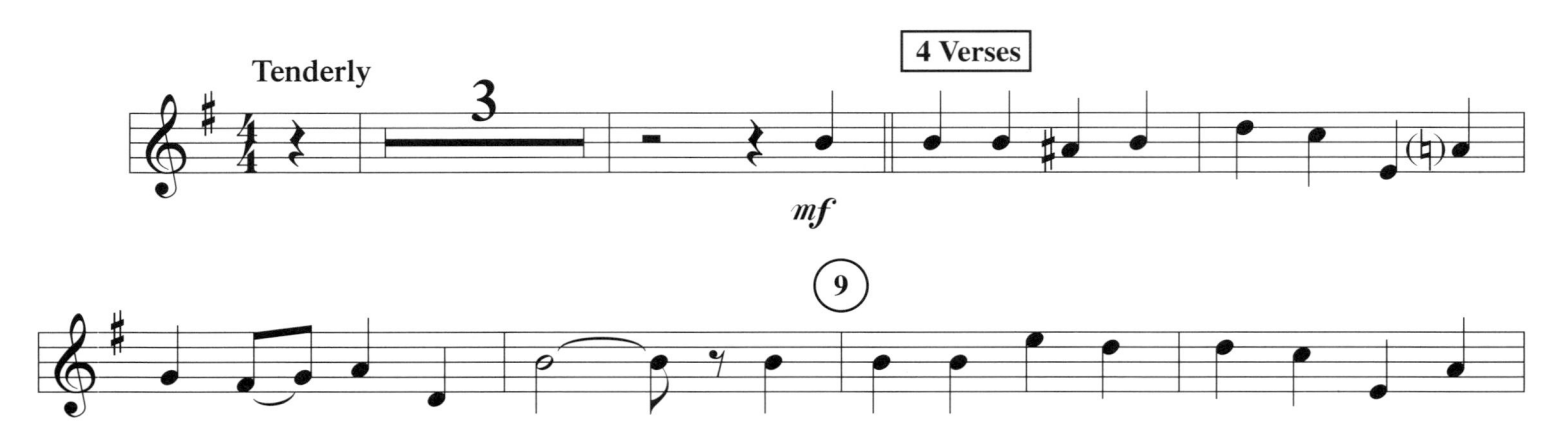

Arr. © 2002 by Lillenas Publishing Company (SESAC). All rights reserved.
Administered by The Copyright Company, 1025 16th Avenue South, Nashville, TN 37212.

21

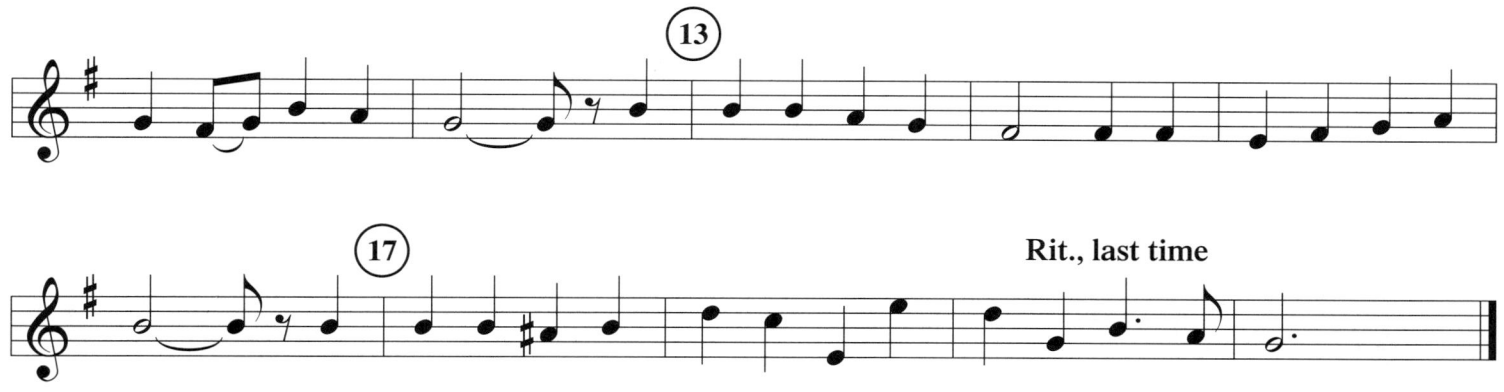

It Came upon the Midnight Clear

Bb Instrument

RICHARD S. WILLIS

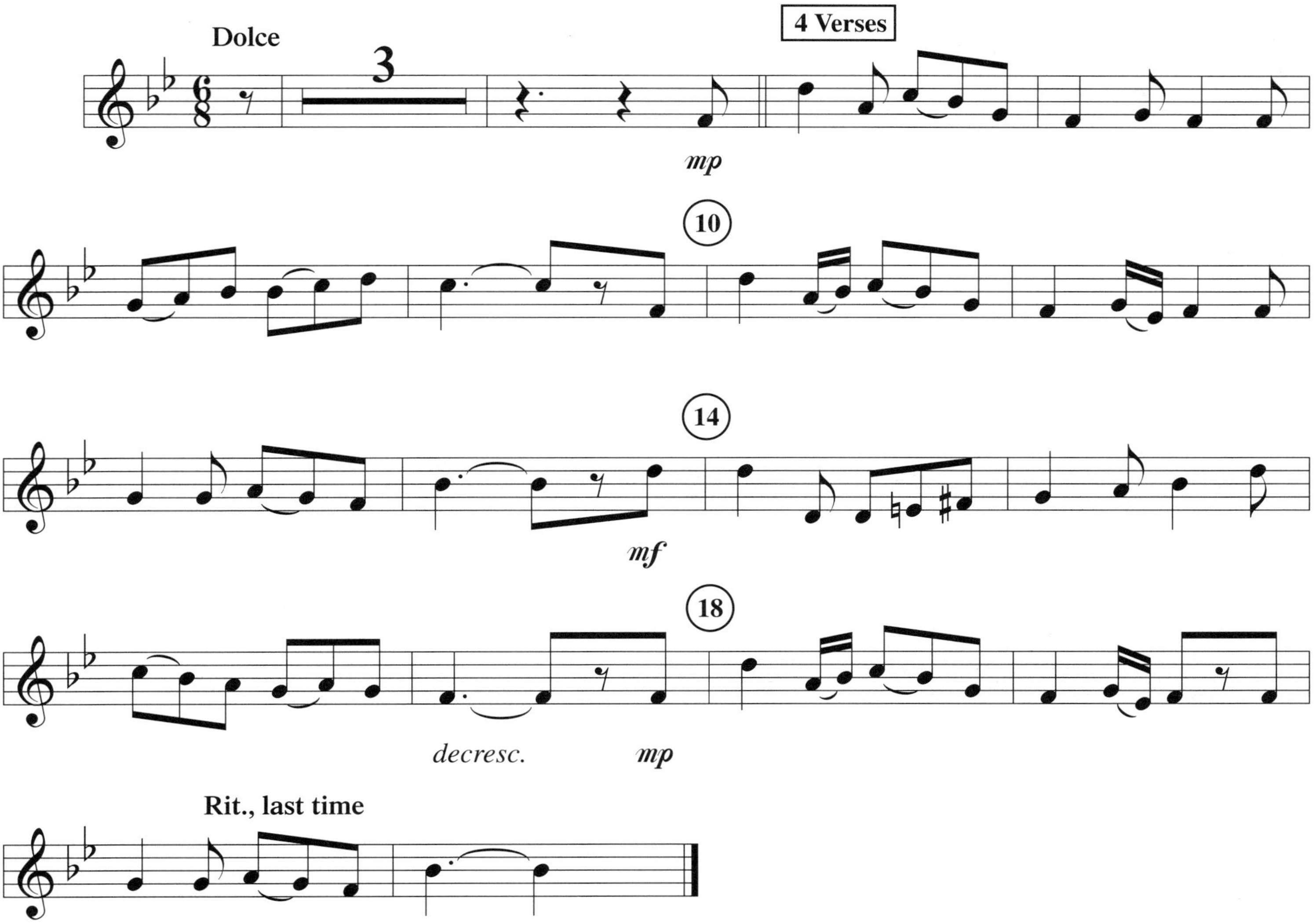

Arr. © 2002 by Lillenas Publishing Company (SESAC). All rights reserved.
Administered by The Copyright Company, 1025 16th Avenue South, Nashville, TN 37212.

Joy to the World

GEORGE FREDERICK HANDEL

Bb Instrument

Joyfully / 4 Verses / *f*

Arr. © 2002 by Lillenas Publishing Company (SESAC). All rights reserved.
Administered by The Copyright Company, 1025 16th Avenue South, Nashville, TN 37212.

O Come, All Ye Faithful

attr. to JOHN F. WADE

Bb Instrument

Jubilantly / 3 Verses / *mf*

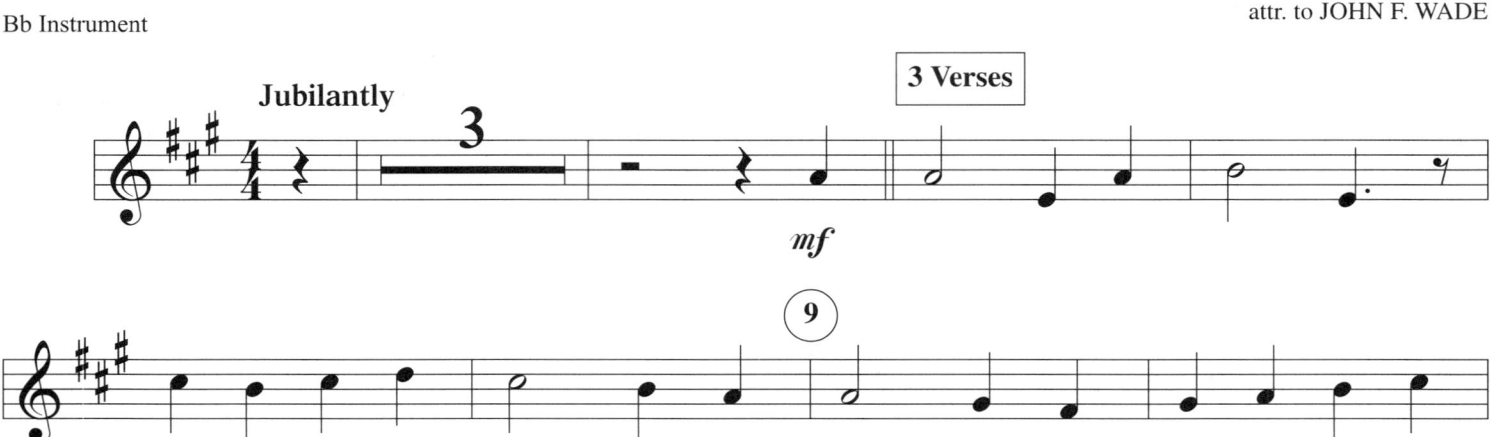

Arr. © 2002 by Lillenas Publishing Company (SESAC). All rights reserved.
Administered by The Copyright Company, 1025 16th Avenue South, Nashville, TN 37212.

Away in a Manger

Bb Instrument

JAMES R. MURRAY

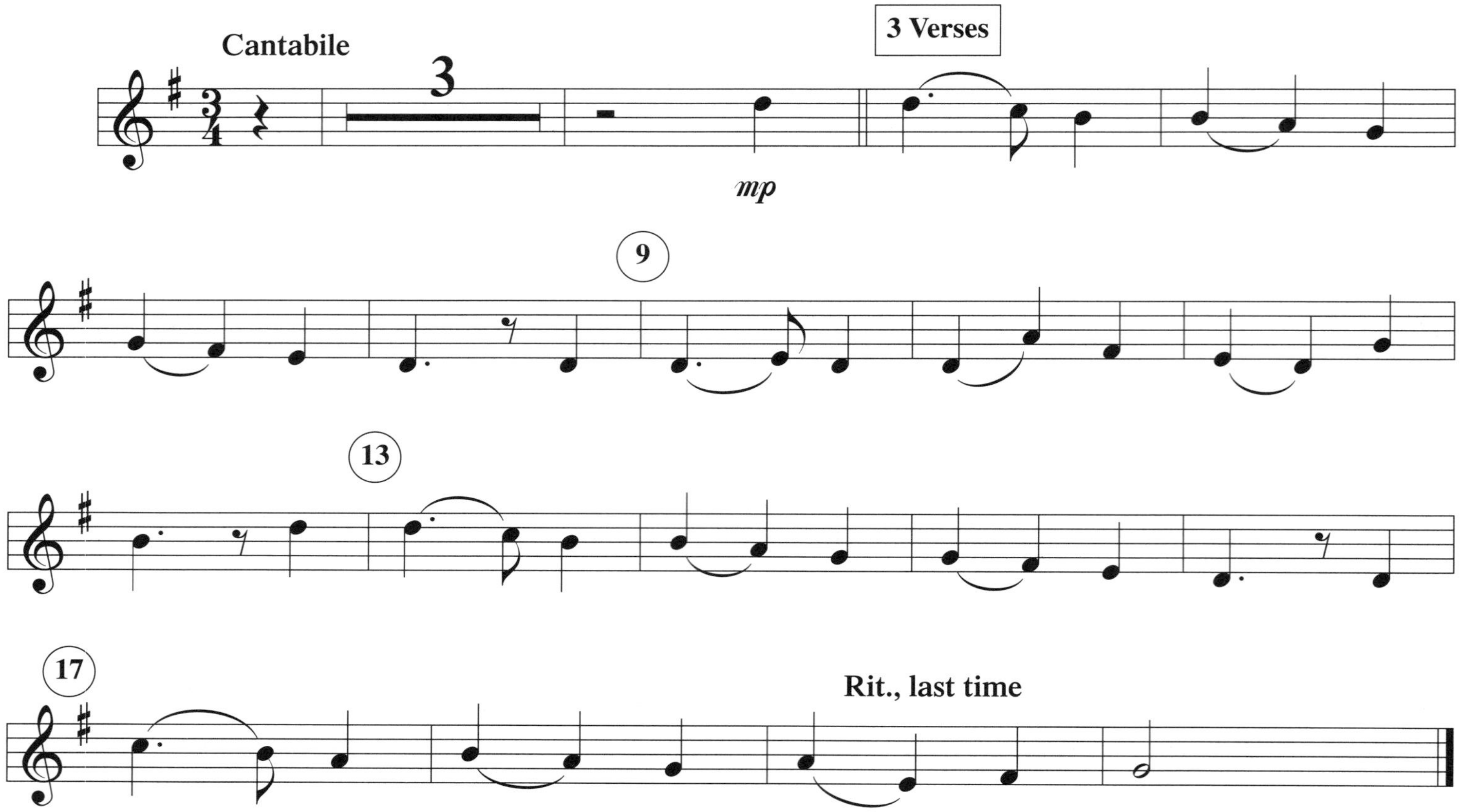

What Child Is This?

Bb Instrument

TRADITIONAL ENGLISH MELODY

25

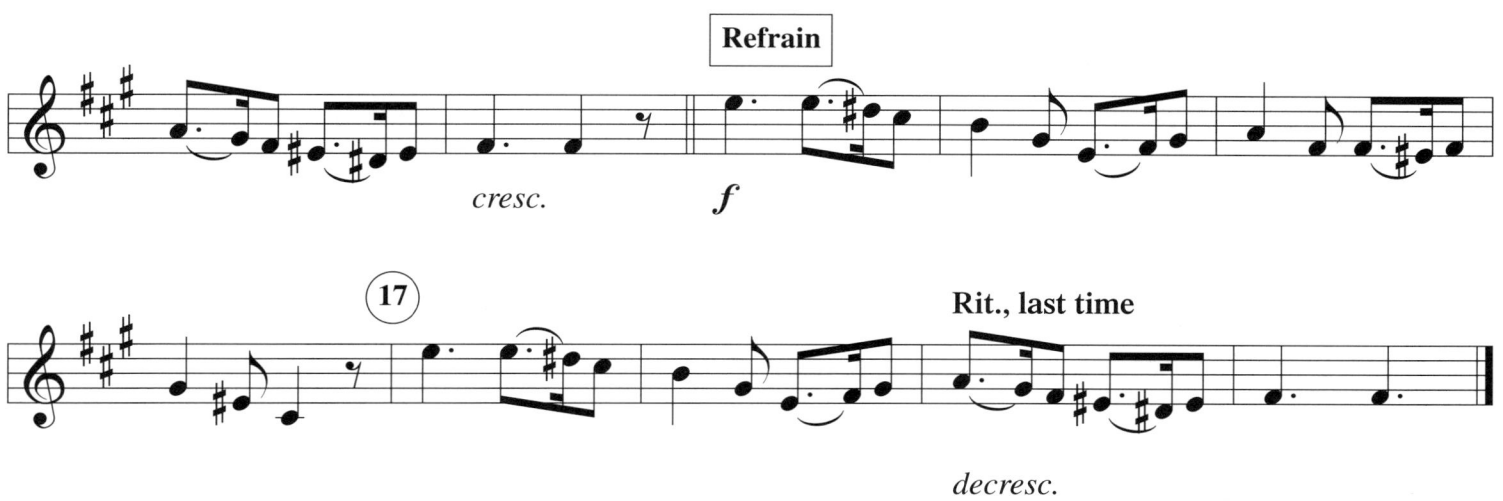

While Shepherds Watched Their Flocks

Bb Instrument

GEORGE FREDERICK HANDEL

Arr. © 2002 by Lillenas Publishing Company (SESAC). All rights reserved.
Administered by The Copyright Company, 1025 16th Avenue South, Nashville, TN 37212.

The First Noel

F Instrument

W. SANDYS' CHRISTMAS CAROLS

Arrangements of
10 Christmas Favorites for

Volume 5

INSTRUMENTAL HYMN SOLOS

Three Accompaniment Options:
● Keyboard   ● CD trax   ● MIDI

LEVEL—MODERATE

Piano (Insert section)

Away in the Manger	15a
It Came upon the Midnight Clear	7a
Joy to the World	11a
O Come, All Ye Faithful	12a
O Come, O Come, Emmanuel	2a
O Little Town of Bethlehem	8a
Silent Night! Holy Night!	10a
The First Noel	4a
What Child Is This?	16a
While Shepherds Watched Their Flocks	17a

The piano folio is only temporarily stapled to the center of this book.
It is easily removed by a slight pull outward.

Copyright © 2002 by Lillenas Publishing Company. All rights reserved. Litho in U.S.A.

PUBLISHING COMPANY
Kansas City, MO 64141
lillenas.com

O Come, O Come, Emmanuel

PLAINSONG
adapted by Thomas Helmore

Arr. © 2002 by Lillenas Publishing Company (SESAC). All rights reserved.
Administered by The Copyright Company, 1025 16th Avenue South, Nashville, TN 37212.

The First Noel

W. SANDYS' CHRISTMAS CAROLS

It Came upon the Midnight Clear

RICHARD S. WILLIS

Arr. © 2002 by Lillenas Publishing Company (SESAC). All rights reserved.
Administered by The Copyright Company, 1025 16th Avenue South, Nashville, TN 37212.

O Little Town of Bethlehem

LEWIS H. REDNER

Arr. © 2002 by Lillenas Publishing Company (SESAC). All rights reserved.
Administered by The Copyright Company, 1025 16th Avenue South, Nashville, TN 37212.

Silent Night! Holy Night!

FRANZ GRUBER

Arr. © 2002 by Lillenas Publishing Company (SESAC). All rights reserved.
Administered by The Copyright Company, 1025 16th Avenue South, Nashville, TN 37212.

Joy to the World

GEORGE FREDERICK HANDEL

O Come, All Ye Faithful

attr. to JOHN F. WADE

13a

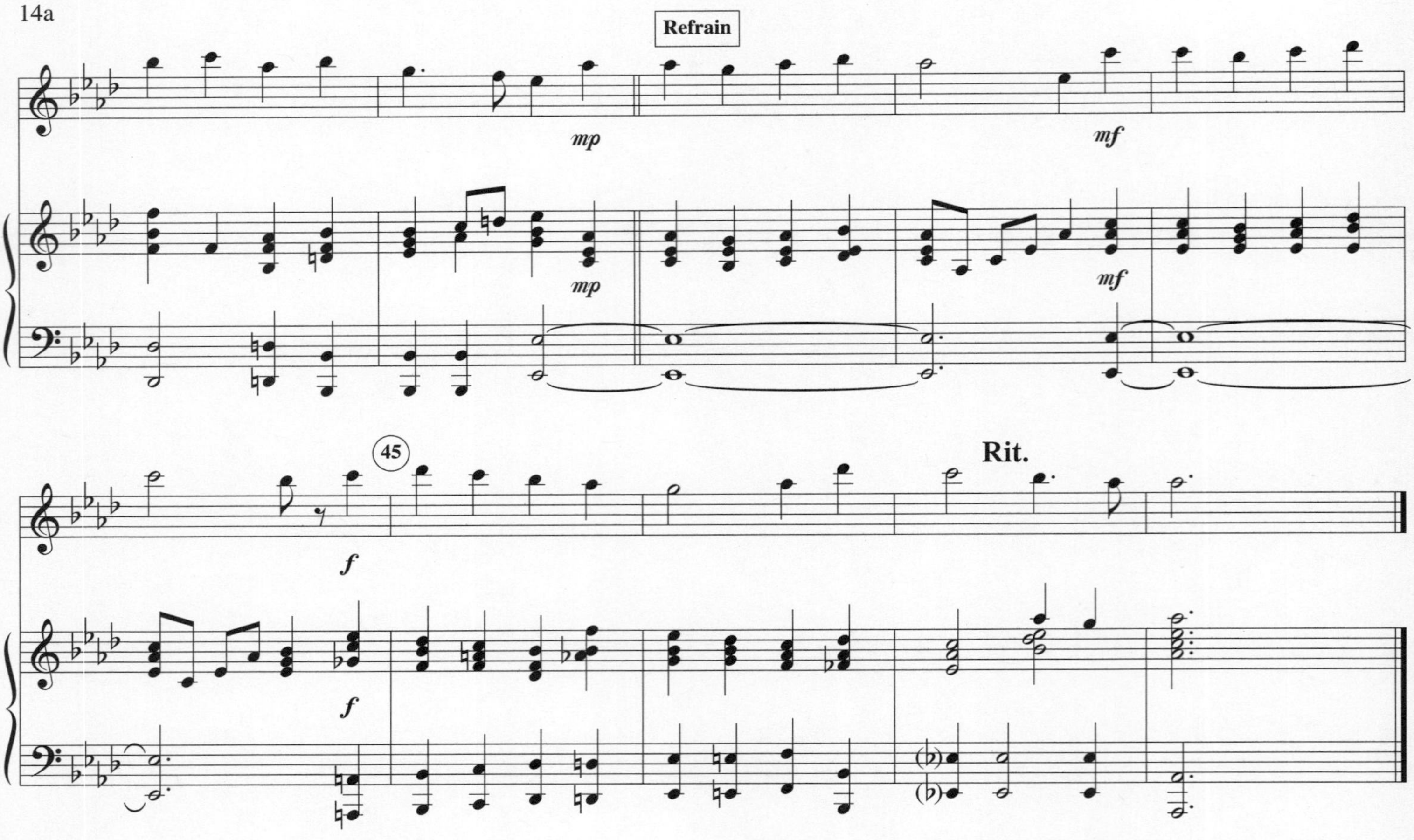

Refrain
mp
mf
mp
mf
45
Rit.
f
f

Away in a Manger

JAMES R. MURRAY

What Child Is This?

TRADITIONAL ENGLISH MELODY

While Shepherds Watched Their Flocks

GEORGE FREDERICK HANDEL

INSTRUMENTAL HYMN SOLOS
Volume 5

Lillenas

MB-879

Silent Night! Holy Night!

FRANZ GRUBER

F Instrument

Arr. © 2002 by Lillenas Publishing Company (SESAC). All rights reserved.
Administered by The Copyright Company, 1025 16th Avenue South, Nashville, TN 37212.

O Come, O Come, Emmanuel

F Instrument

PLAINSONG
adapted by Thomas Helmore

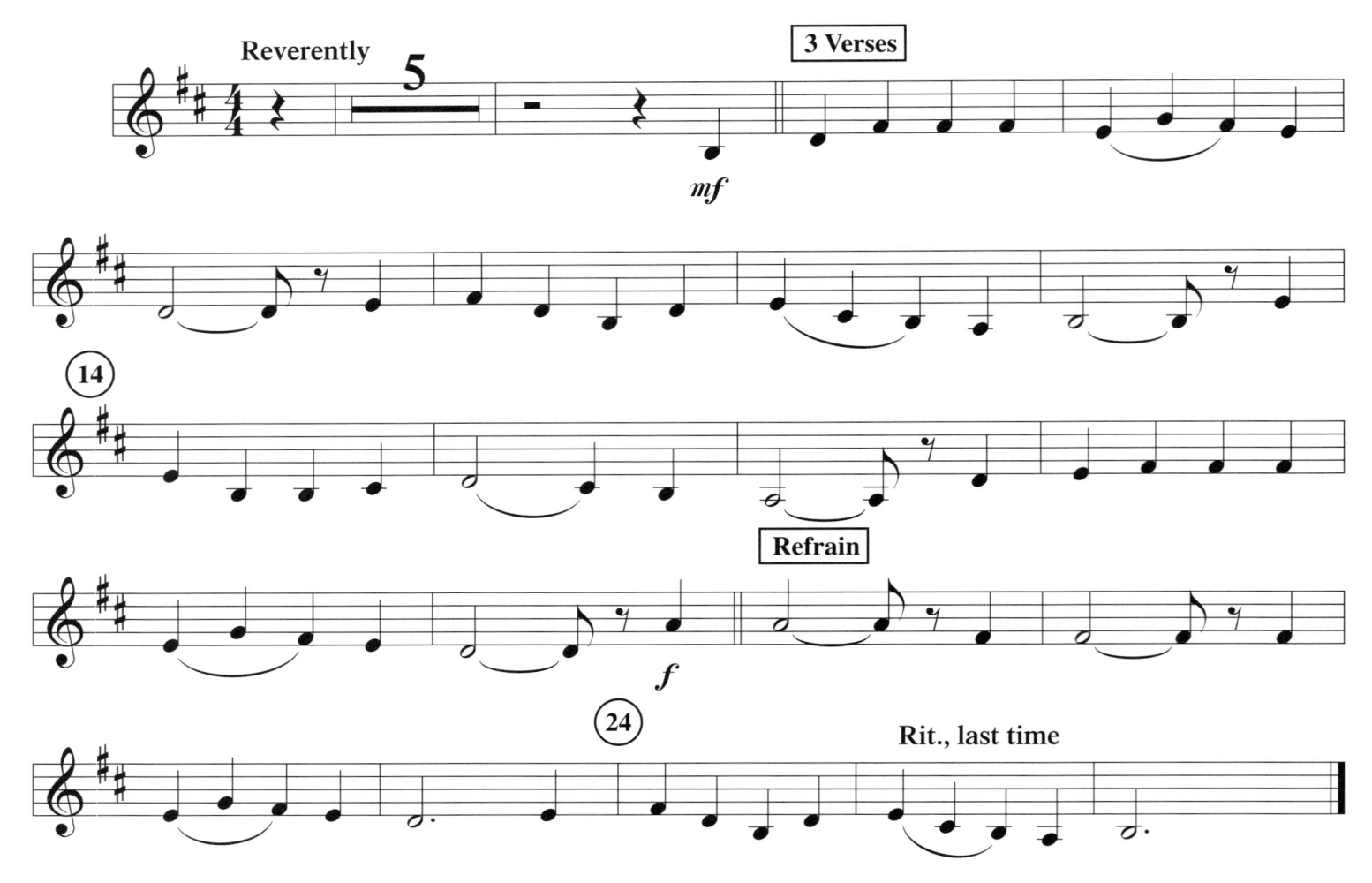

O Little Town of Bethlehem

F Instrument

LEWIS H. REDNER

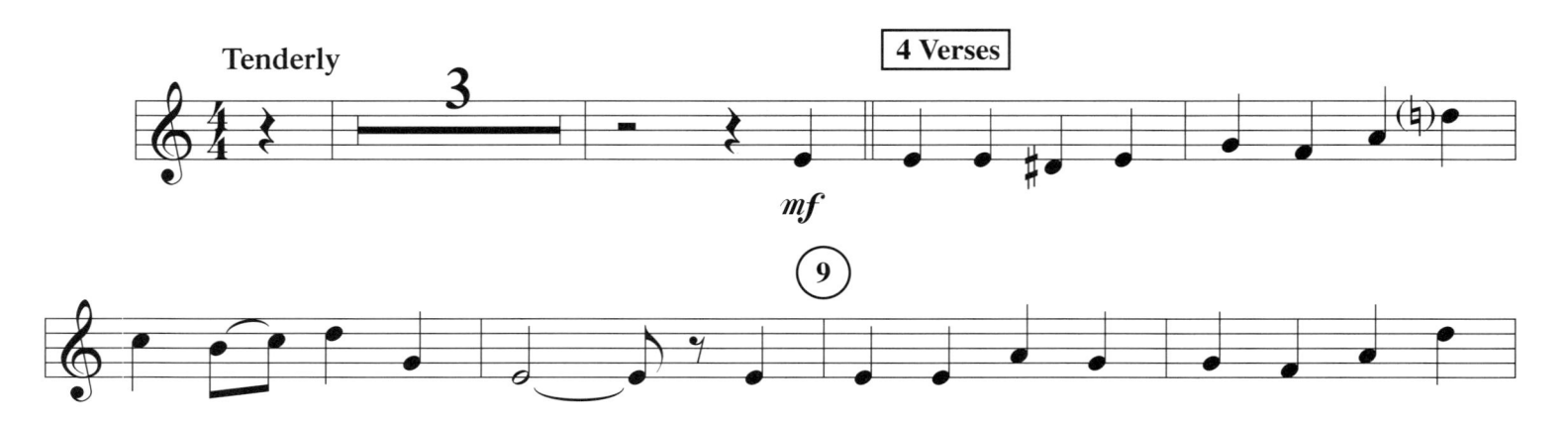

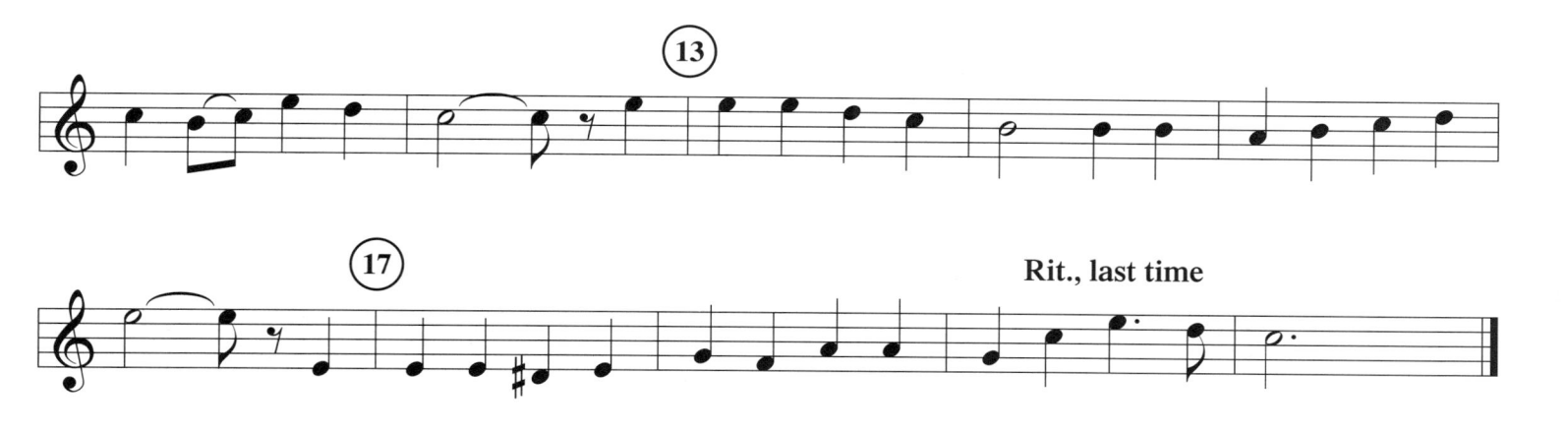

It Came upon the Midnight Clear

F Instrument

RICHARD S. WILLIS

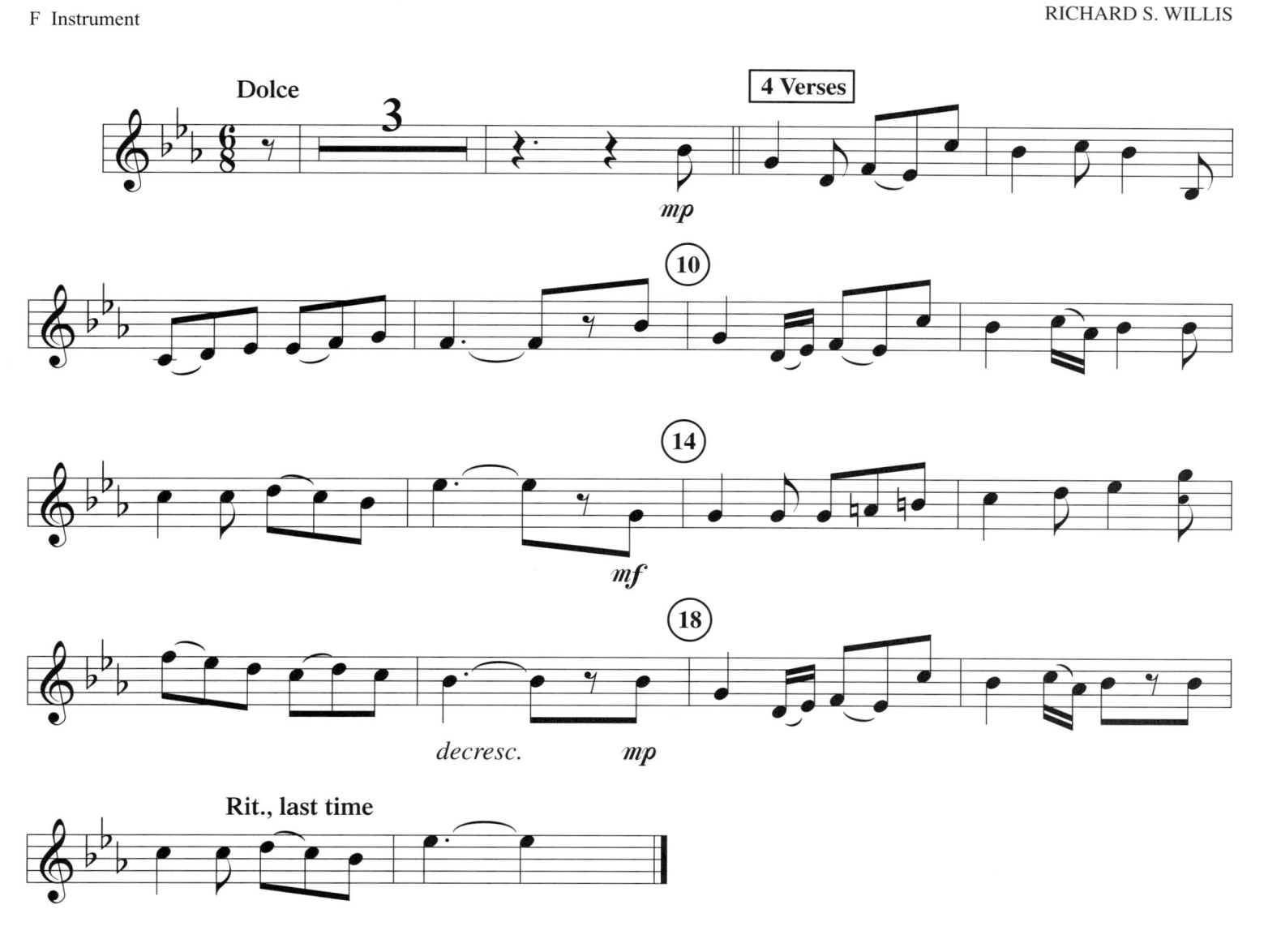

Joy to the World

GEORGE FREDERICK HANDEL

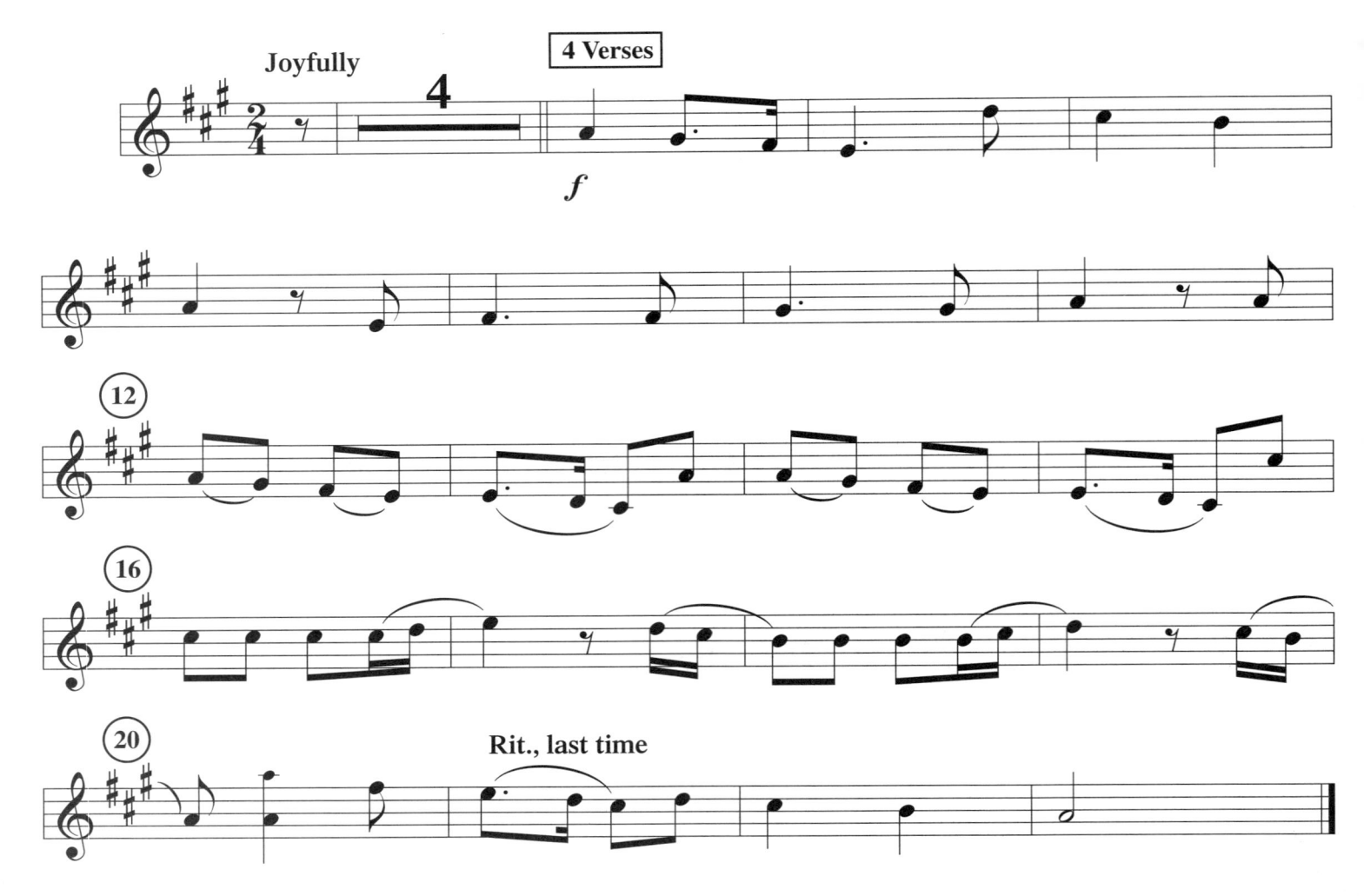

F Instrument

Joyfully

4 Verses

Arr. © 2002 by Lillenas Publishing Company (SESAC). All rights reserved.
Administered by The Copyright Company, 1025 16th Avenue South, Nashville, TN 37212.

O Come, All Ye Faithful

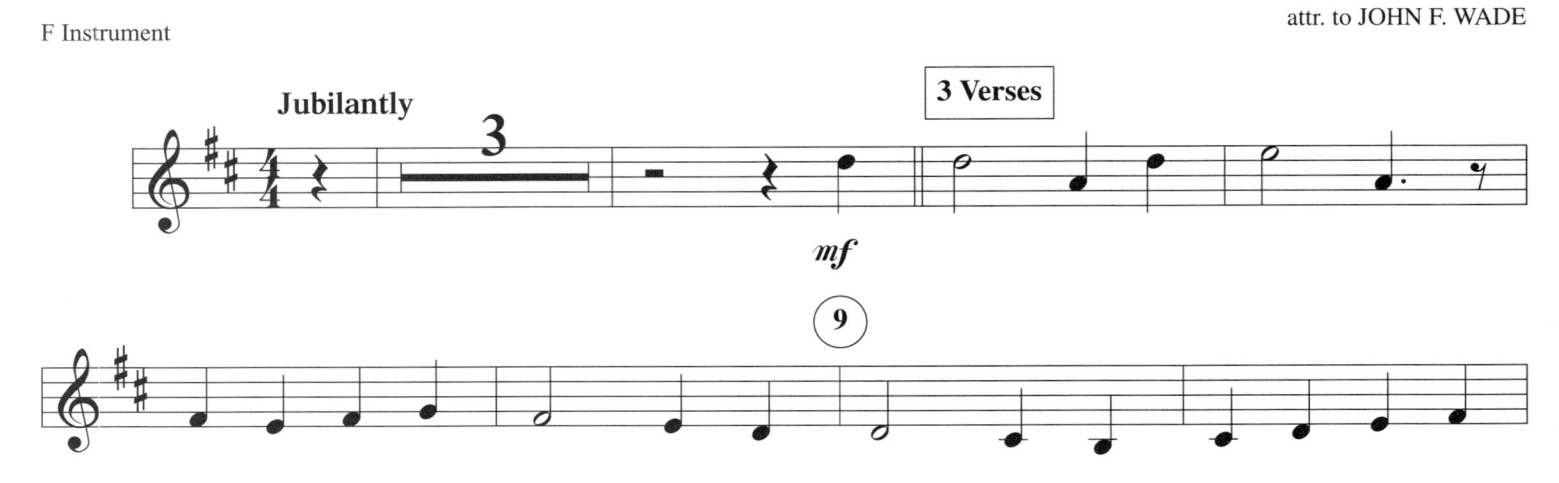

attr. to JOHN F. WADE

F Instrument

Jubilantly

3 Verses

Arr. © 2002 by Lillenas Publishing Company (SESAC). All rights reserved.
Administered by The Copyright Company, 1025 16th Avenue South, Nashville, TN 37212.

31

Away in a Manger

JAMES R. MURRAY

F Instrument

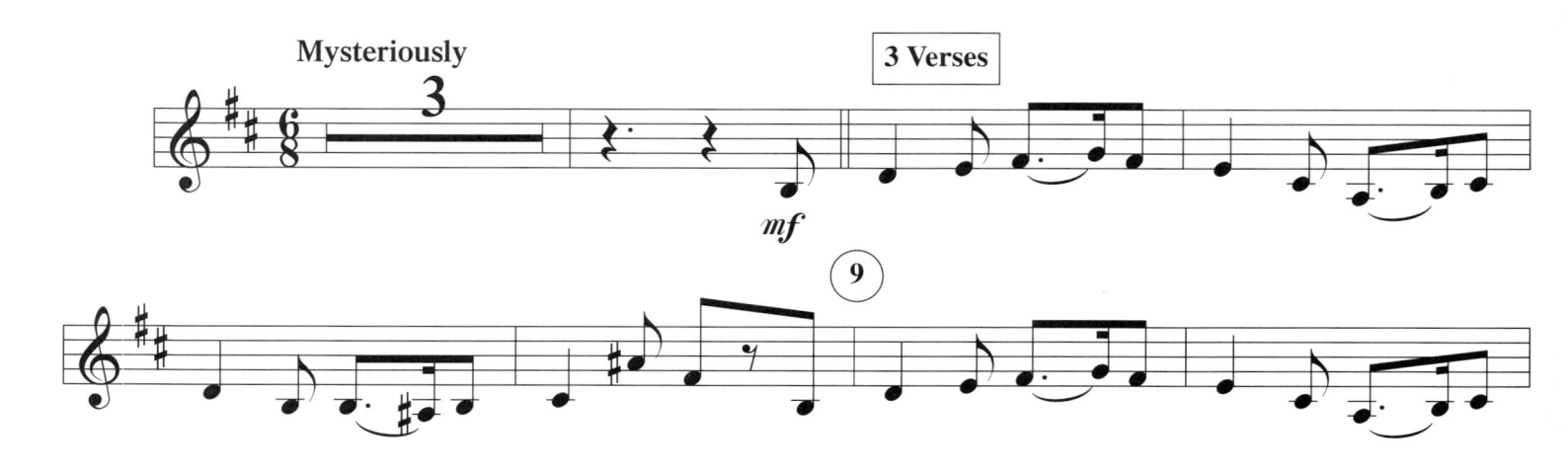

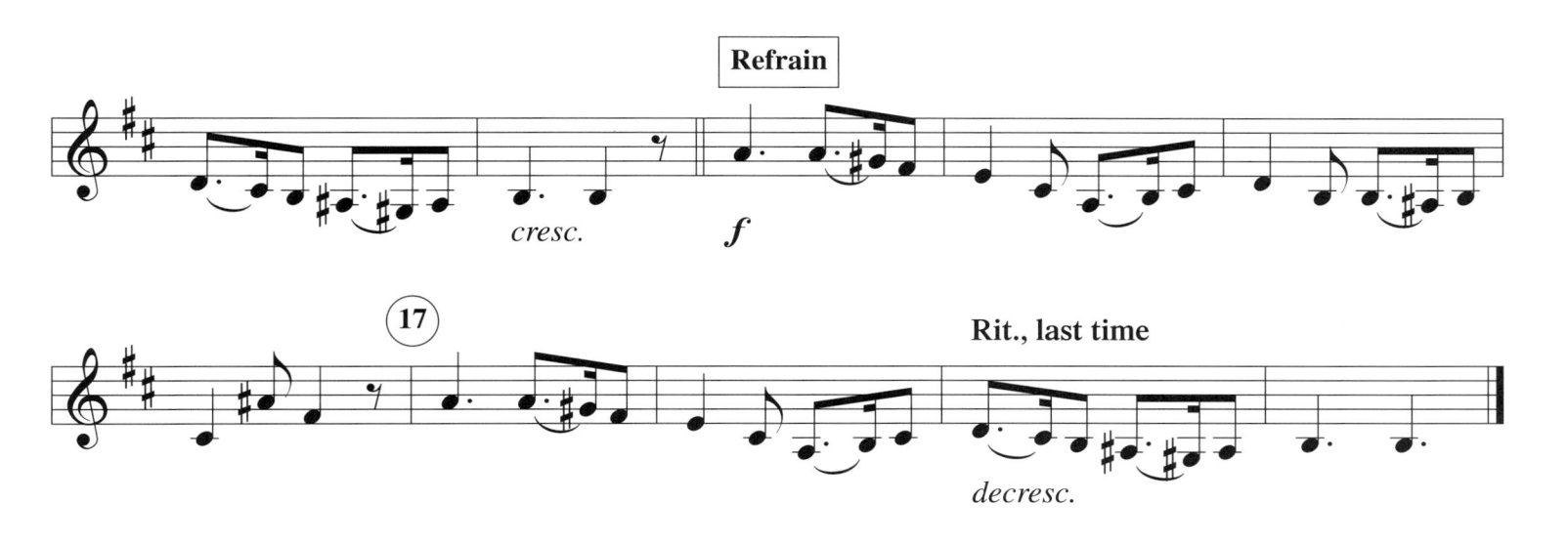

While Shepherds Watched Their Flocks

GEORGE FREDERICK HANDEL

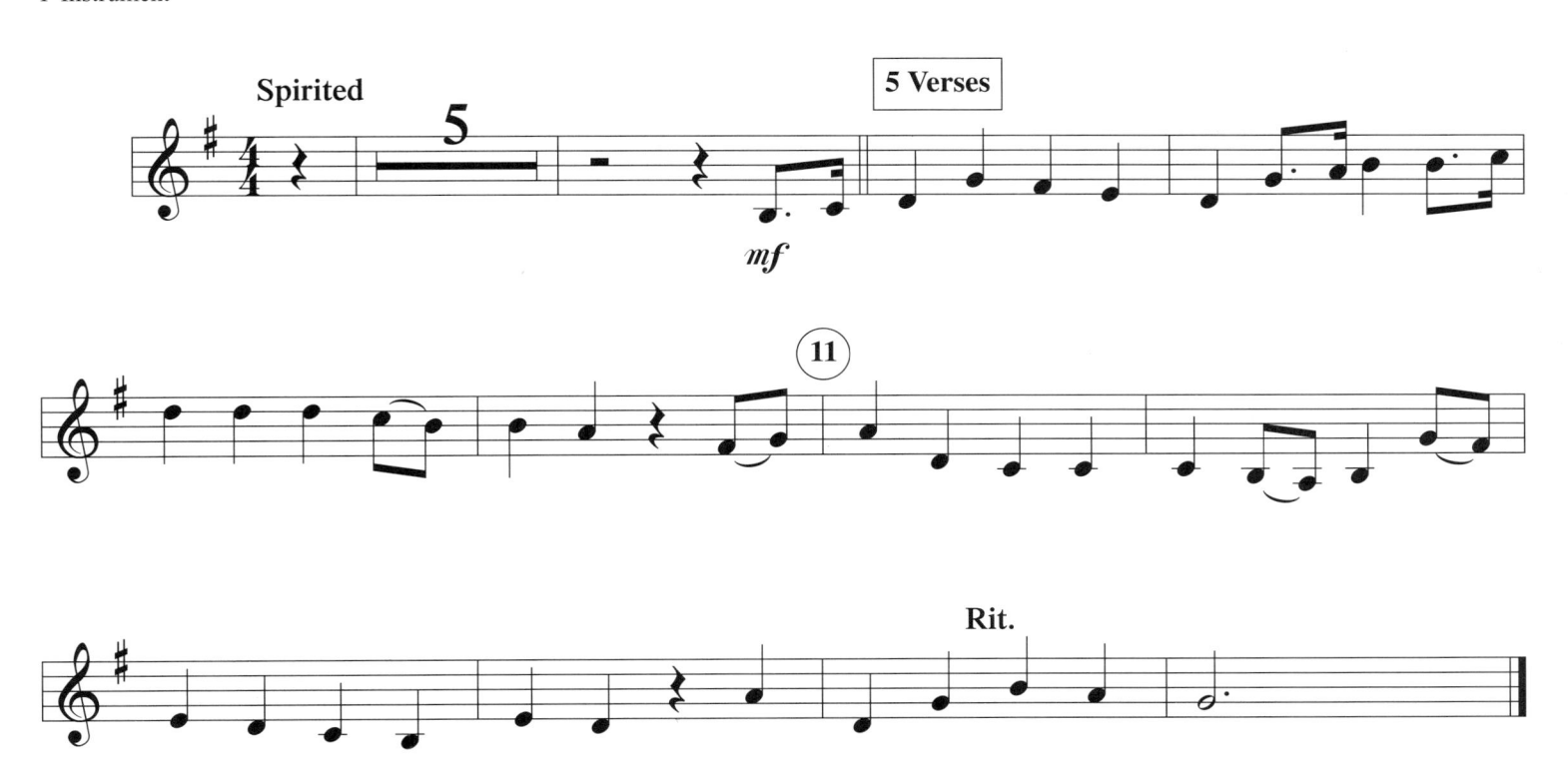

F Instrument

The First Noel

Eb Instrument

W. SANDYS' CHRISTMAS CAROLS

Silent Night! Holy Night!

Eb Instrument

FRANZ GRUBER

O Come, O Come, Emmanuel

Eb Instrument

PLAINSONG
adapted by Thomas Helmore

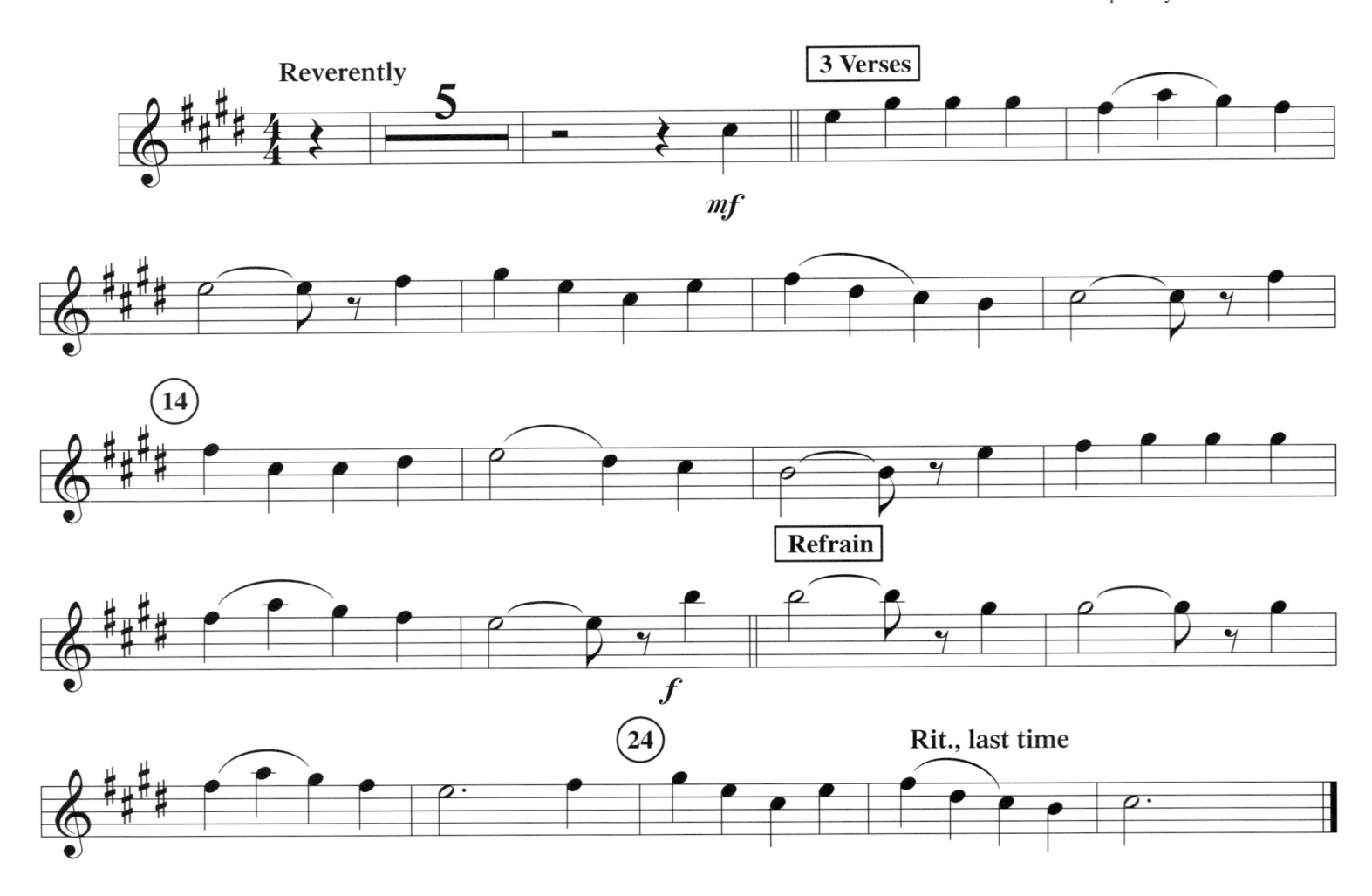

O Little Town of Bethlehem

Eb Instrument

LEWIS H. REDNER

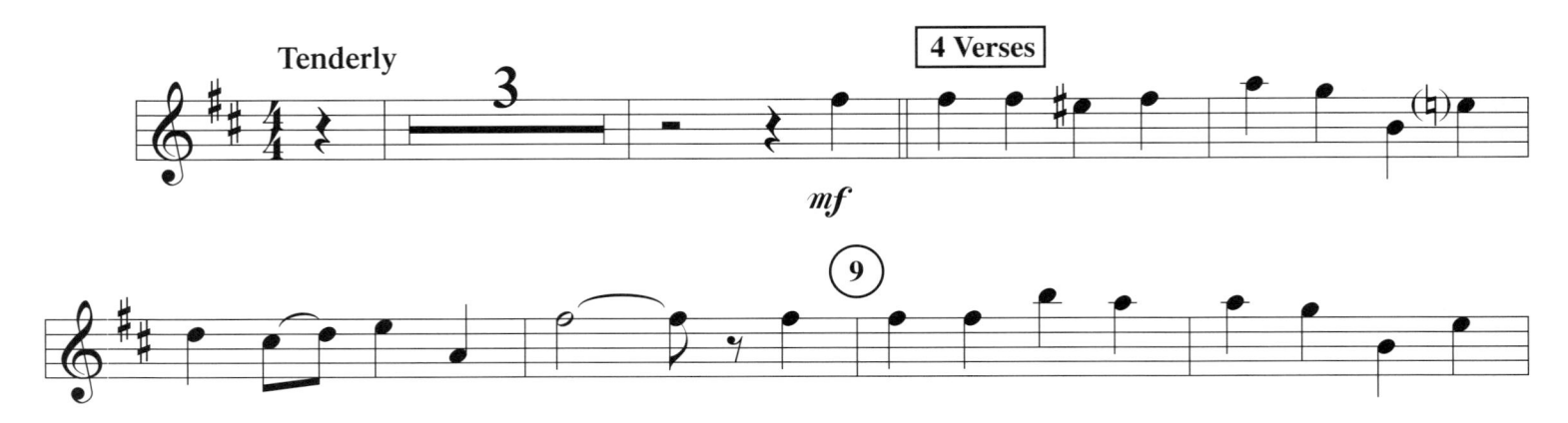

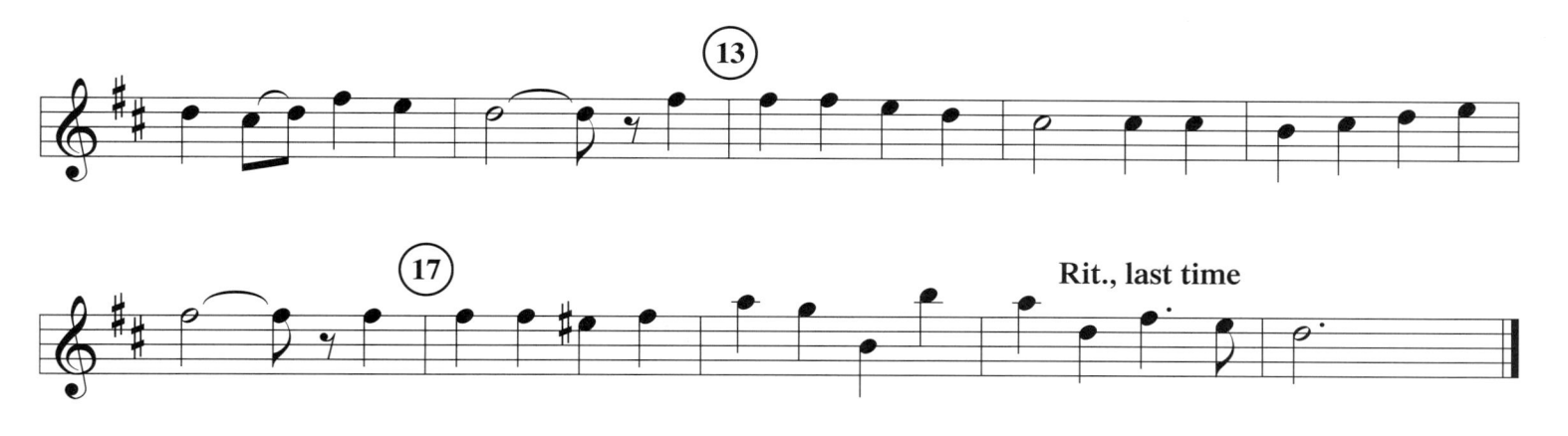

It Came upon the Midnight Clear

Eb Instrument

RICHARD S. WILLIS

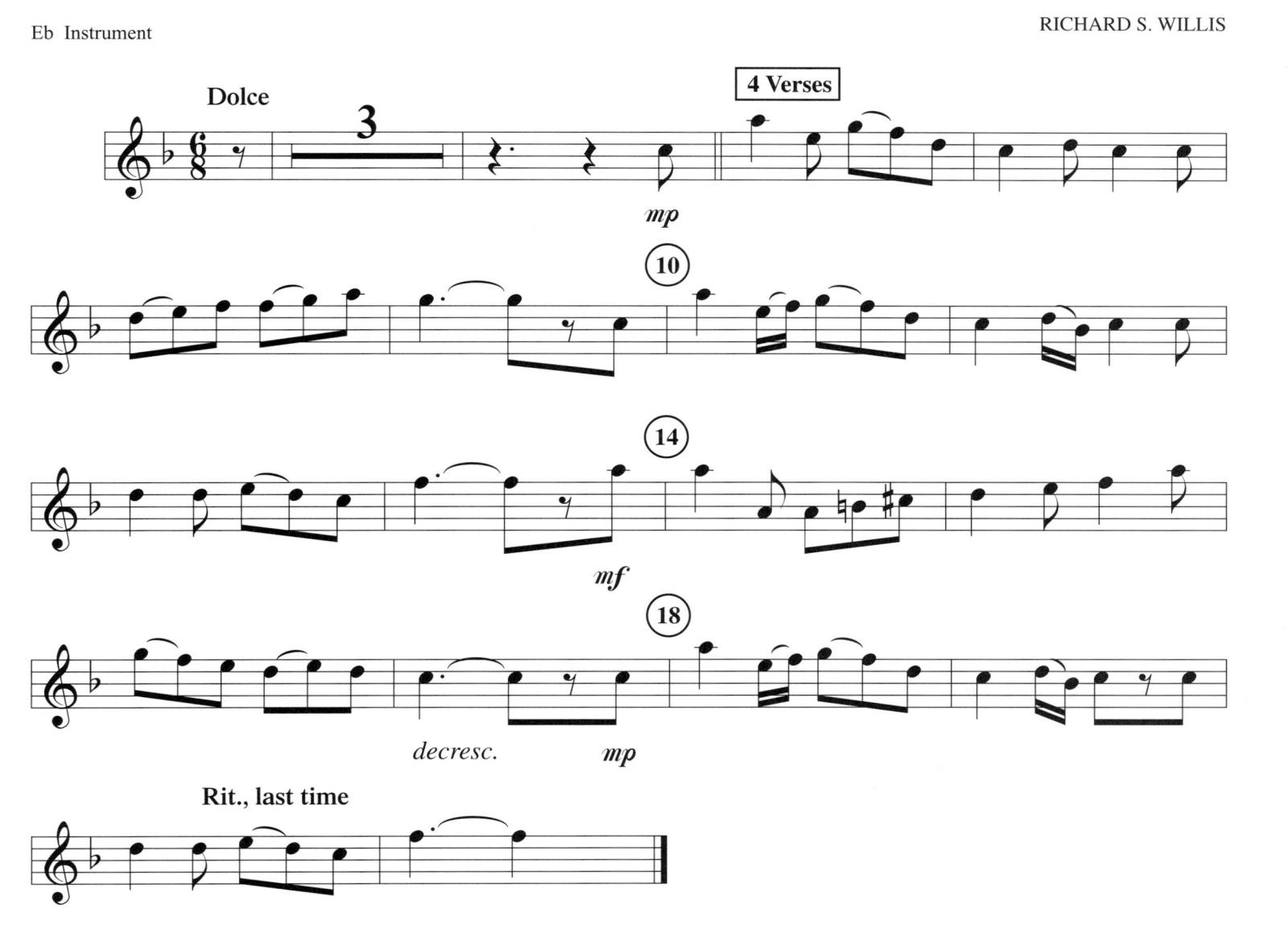

Joy to the World

George Frederick Handel

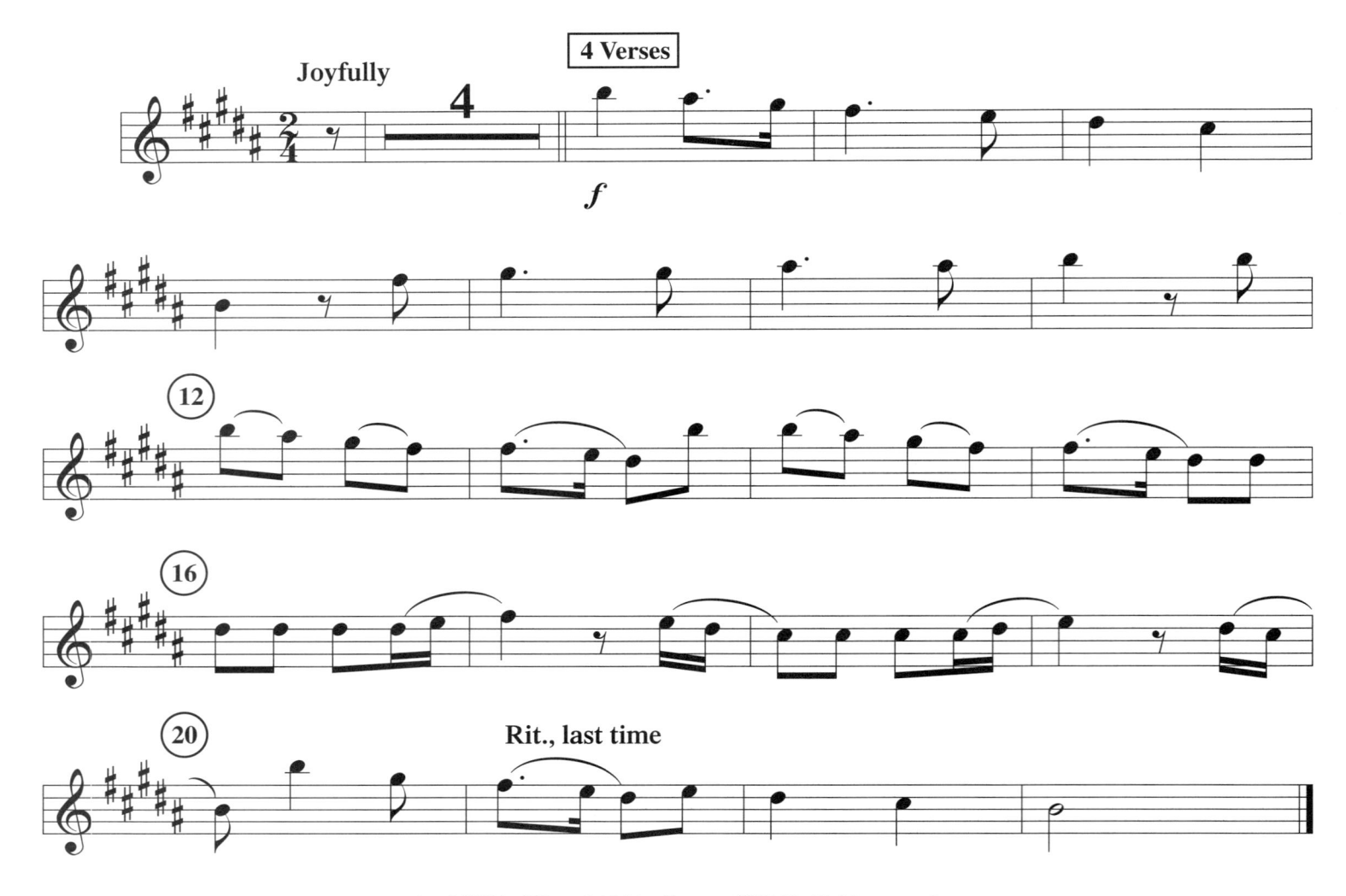

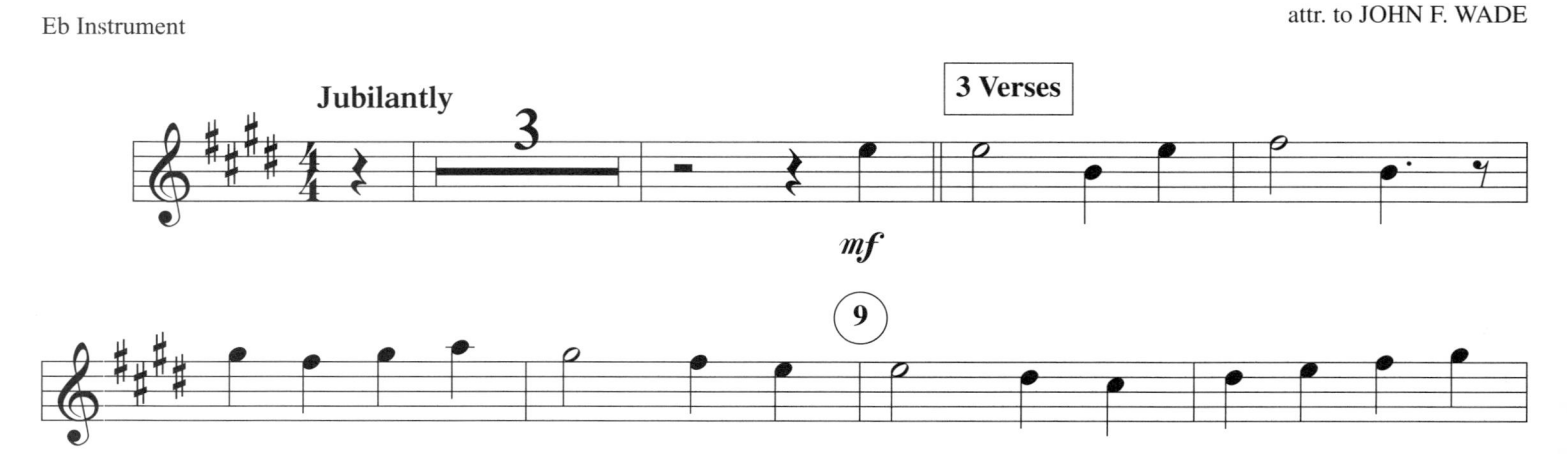

Eb Instrument

Joyfully — 4 Verses

39

Away in a Manger

Eb Instrument

JAMES R. MURRAY

Cantabile — 3 Verses
mp

Rit., last time

Arr. © 2002 by Lillenas Publishing Company (SESAC). All rights reserved.
Administered by The Copyright Company, 1025 16th Avenue South, Nashville, TN 37212.

What Child Is This?

Eb Instrument

TRADITIONAL ENGLISH MELODY

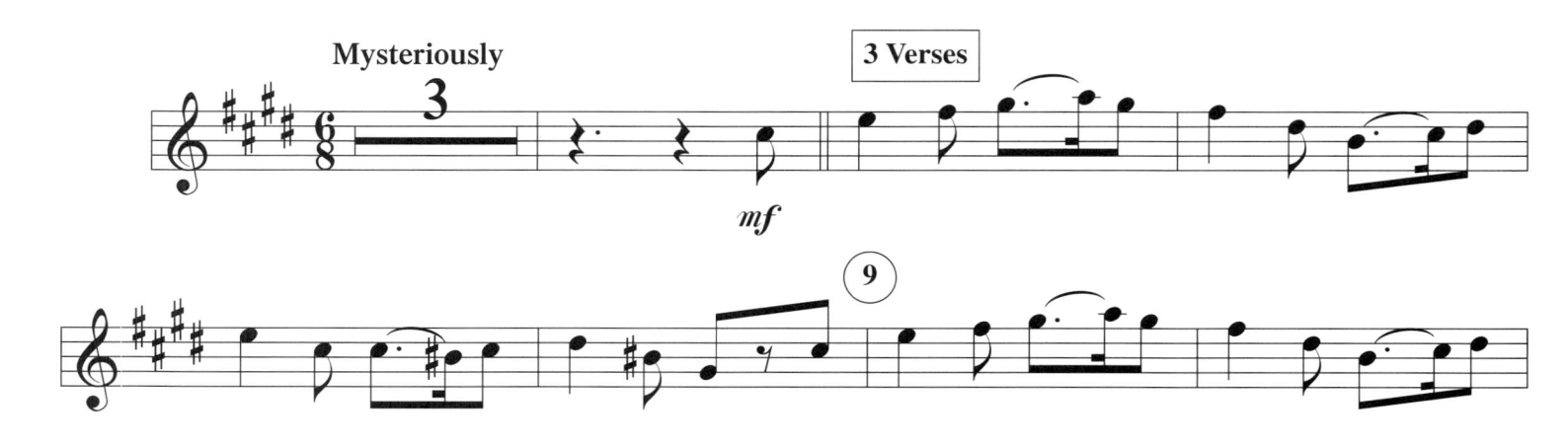

Mysteriously — 3 Verses
mf

Arr. © 2002 by Lillenas Publishing Company (SESAC). All rights reserved.
Administered by The Copyright Company, 1025 16th Avenue South, Nashville, TN 37212.

41

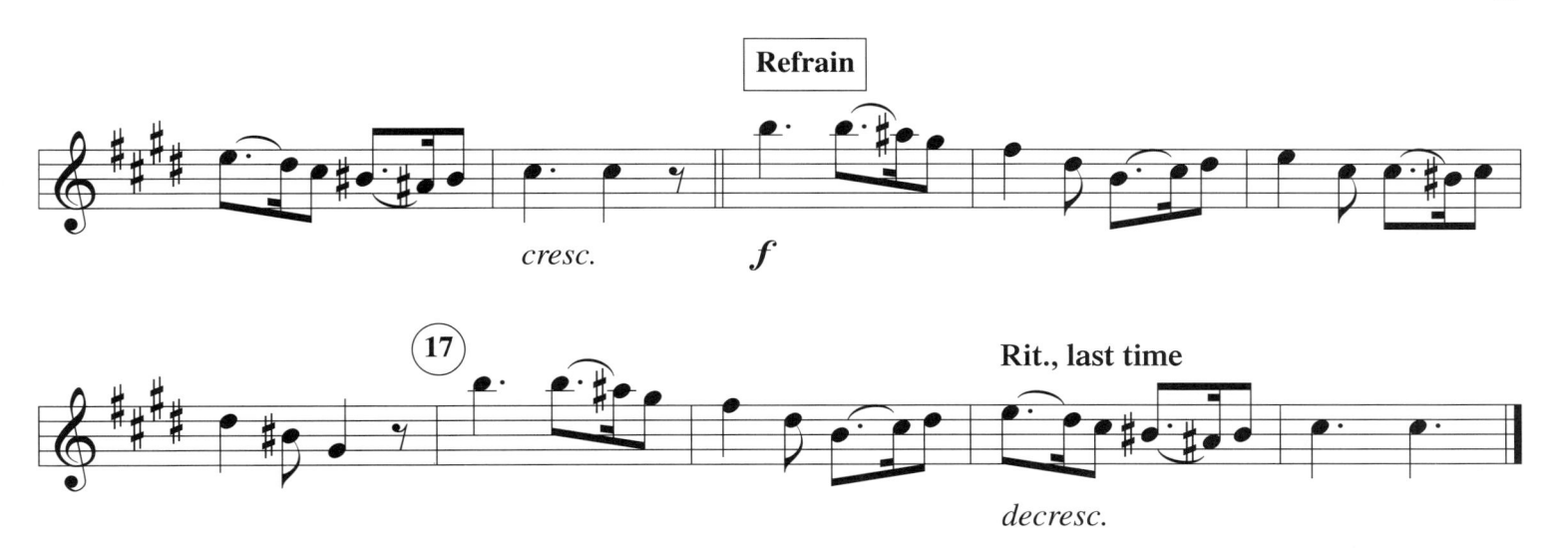

While Shepherds Watched Their Flocks

GEORGE FREDERICK HANDEL

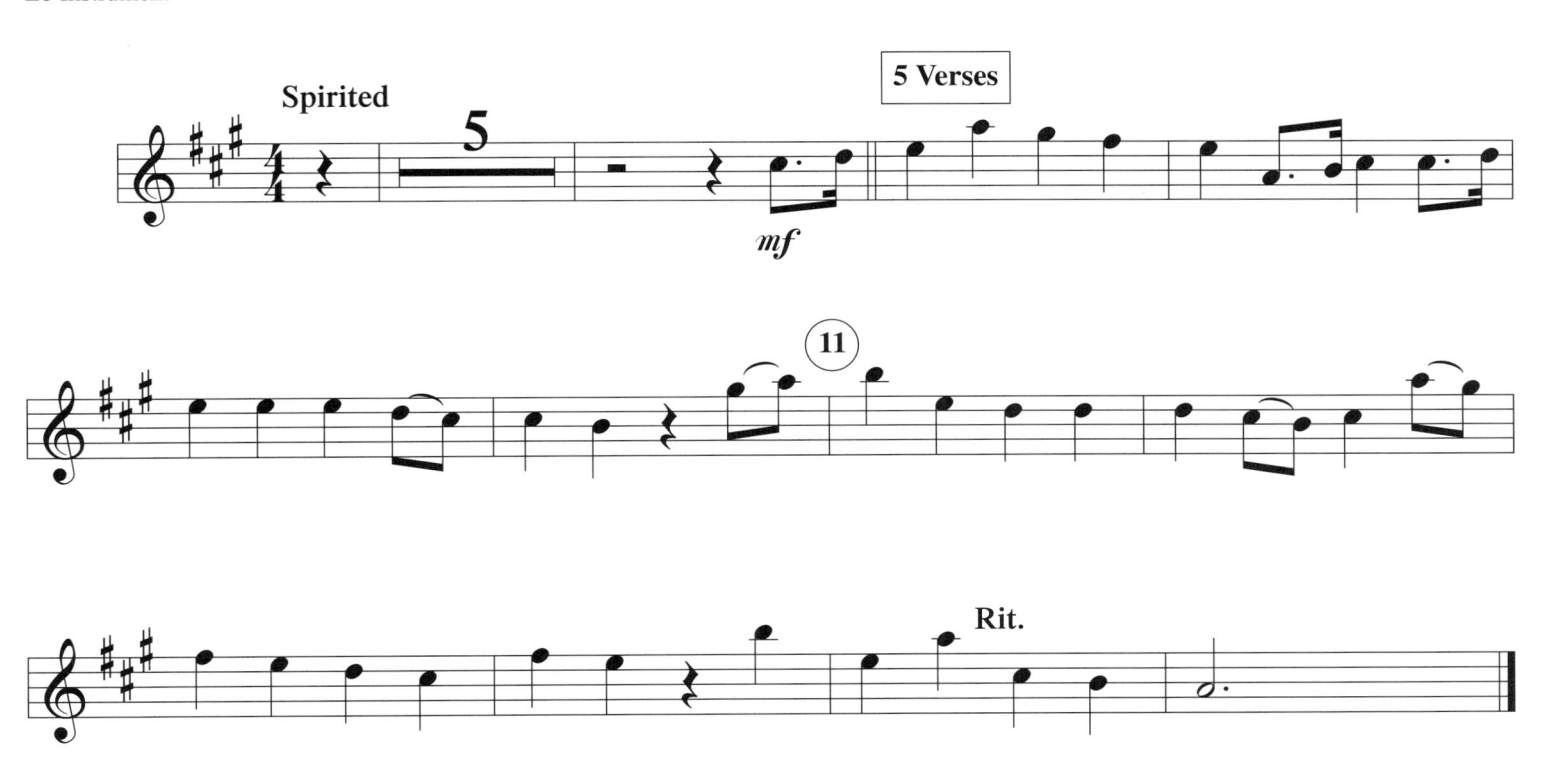

Eb Instrument

Arr. © 2002 by Lillenas Publishing Company (SESAC). All rights reserved.
Administered by The Copyright Company, 1025 16th Avenue South, Nashville, TN 37212.

The First Noel

Alto Clef

W. SANDYS' CHRISTMAS CAROLS

Silent Night! Holy Night!

FRANZ GRUBER

Arr. © 2002 by Lillenas Publishing Company (SESAC). All rights reserved.
Administered by The Copyright Company, 1025 16th Avenue South, Nashville, TN 37212.

O Come, O Come, Emmanuel

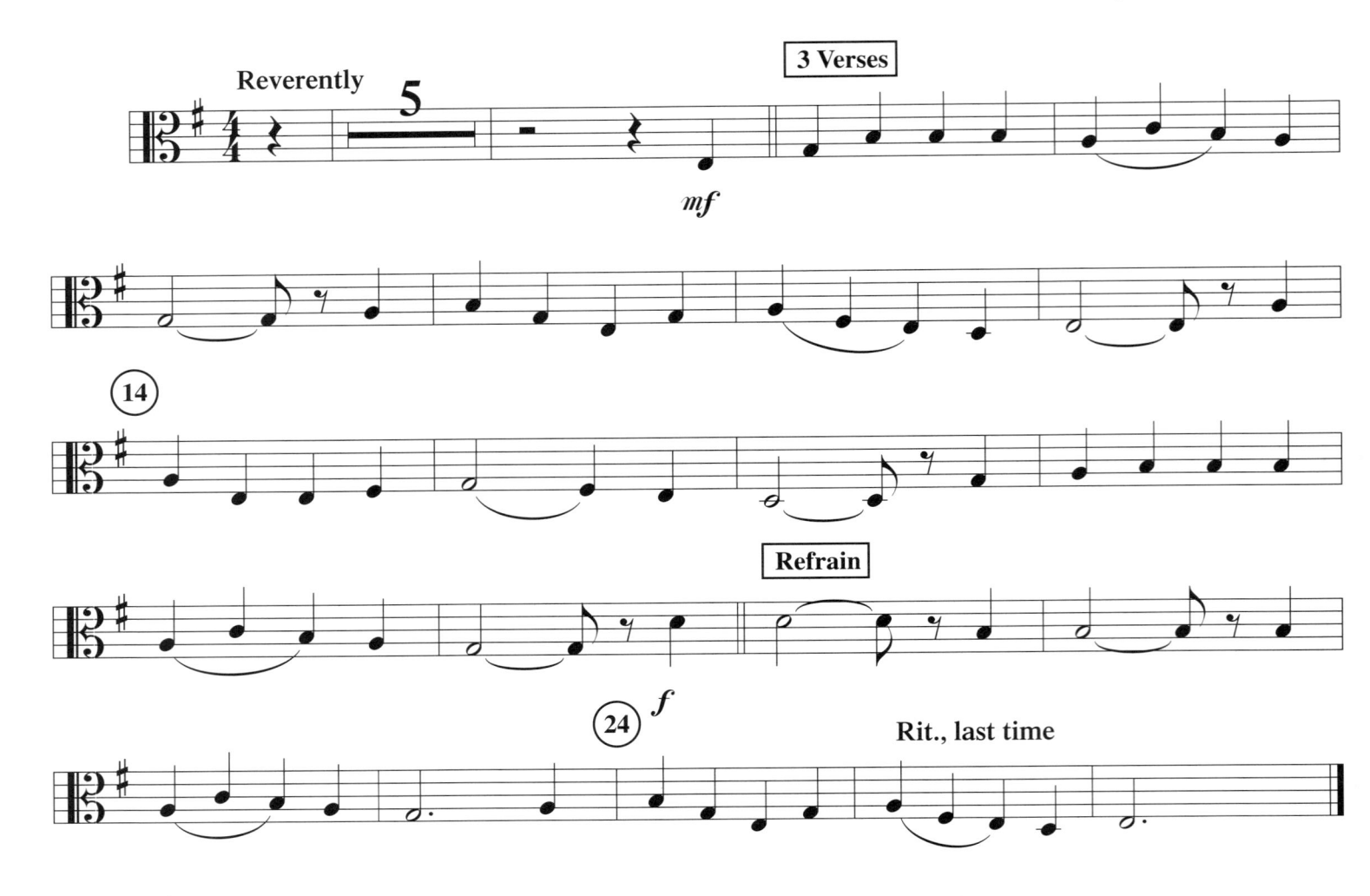

O Little Town of Bethlehem

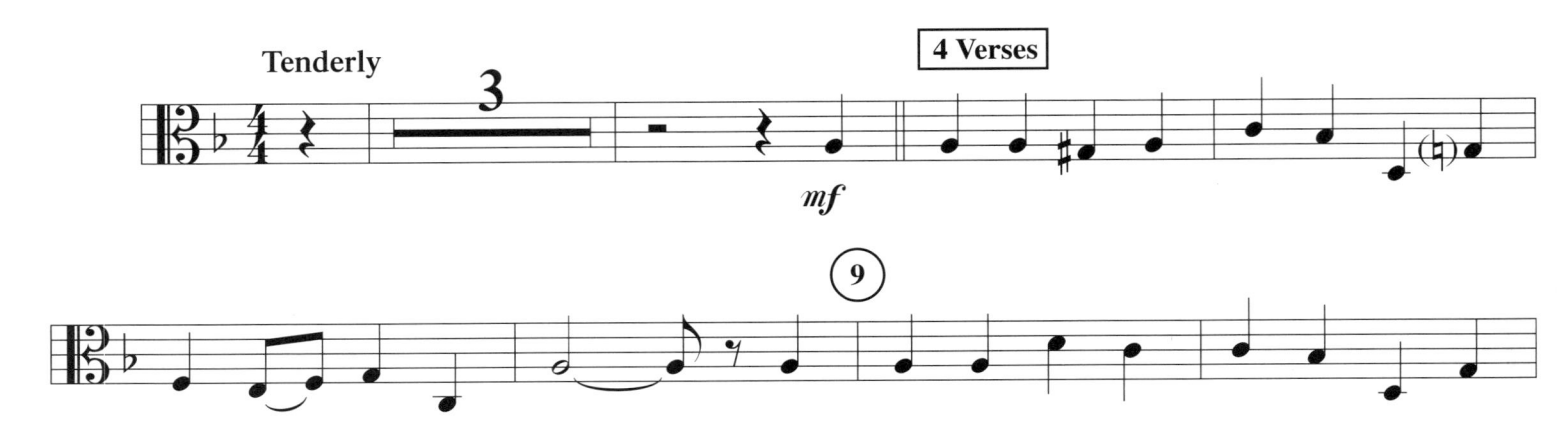

45

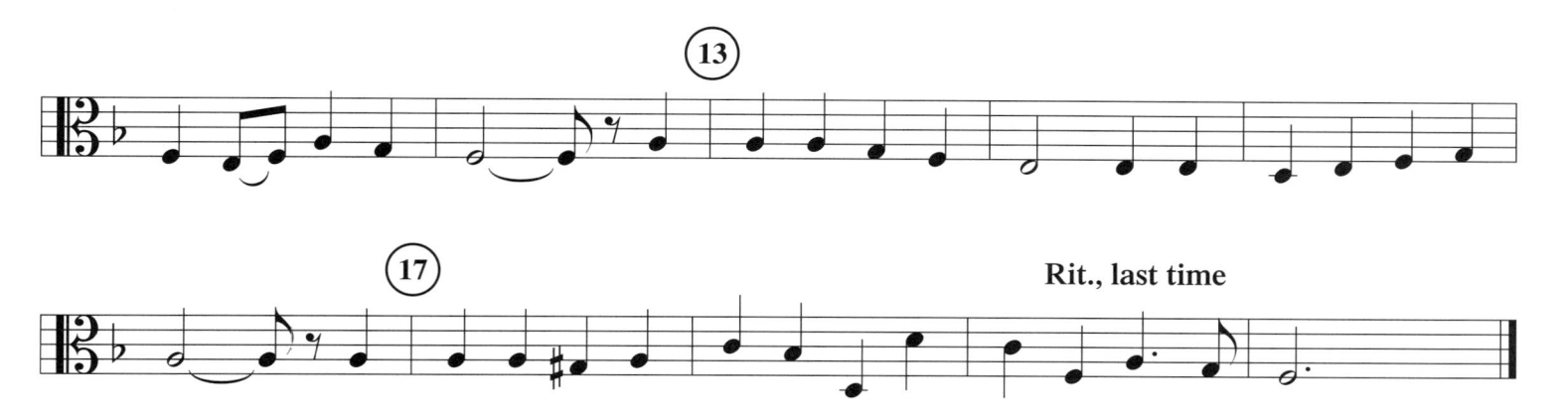

It Came upon the Midnight Clear

Alto Clef

RICHARD S. WILLIS

Arr. © 2002 by Lillenas Publishing Company (SESAC). All rights reserved.
Administered by The Copyright Company, 1025 16th Avenue South, Nashville, TN 37212.

Joy to the World

GEORGE FREDERICK HANDEL

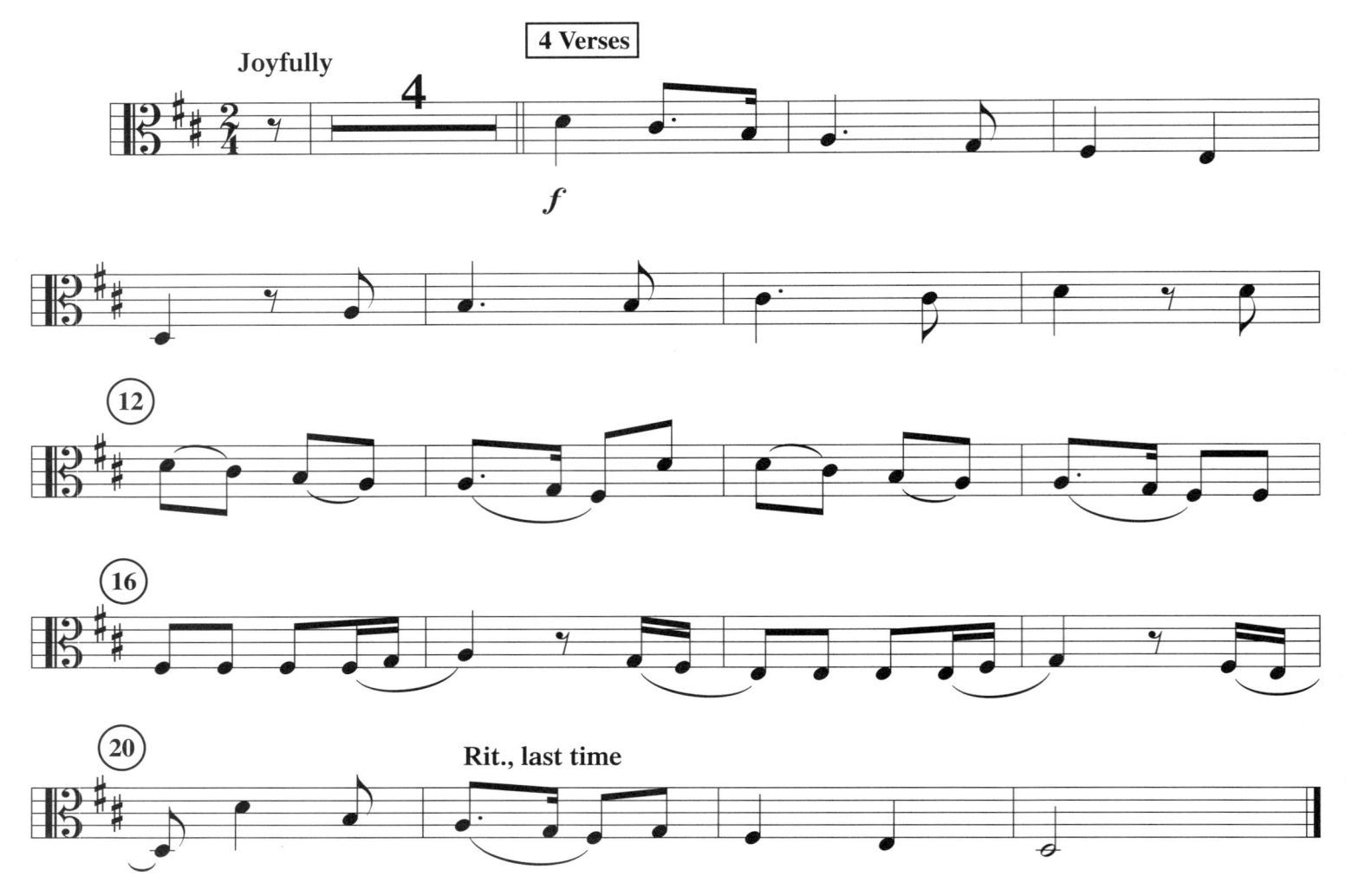

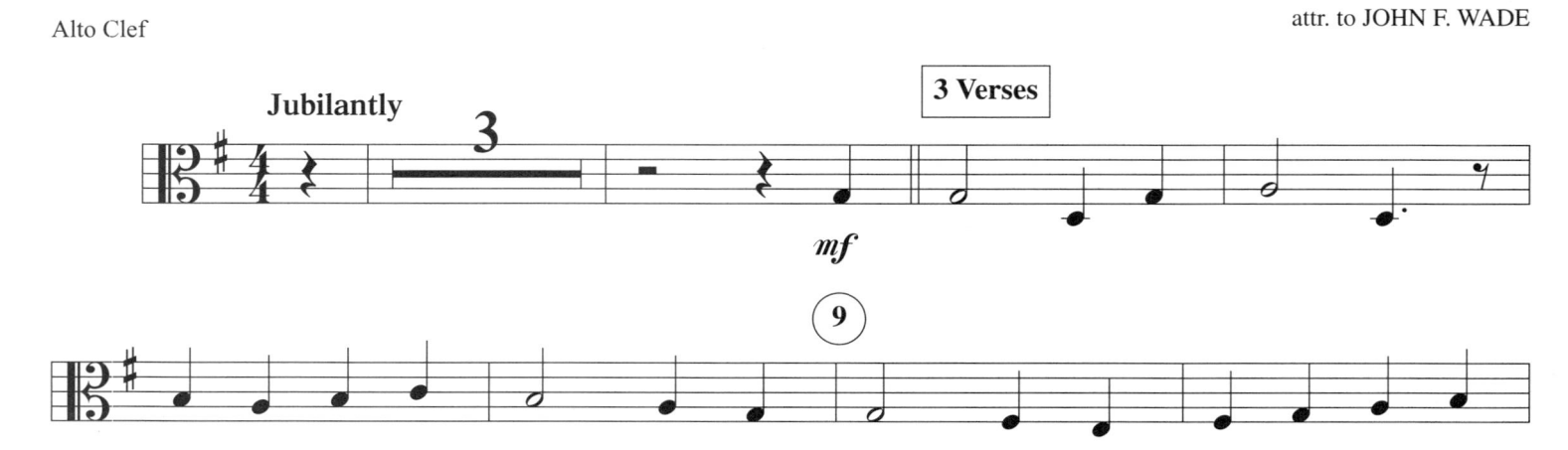

Alto Clef

Joyfully

13
Refrain
mp
21
mf
1
2 (Transition to opt. last verse)
3
29
Broadly
f
33
37
mp
Refrain
mf
f
45
Rit.

Away in a Manger

Alto Clef

JAMES R. MURRAY

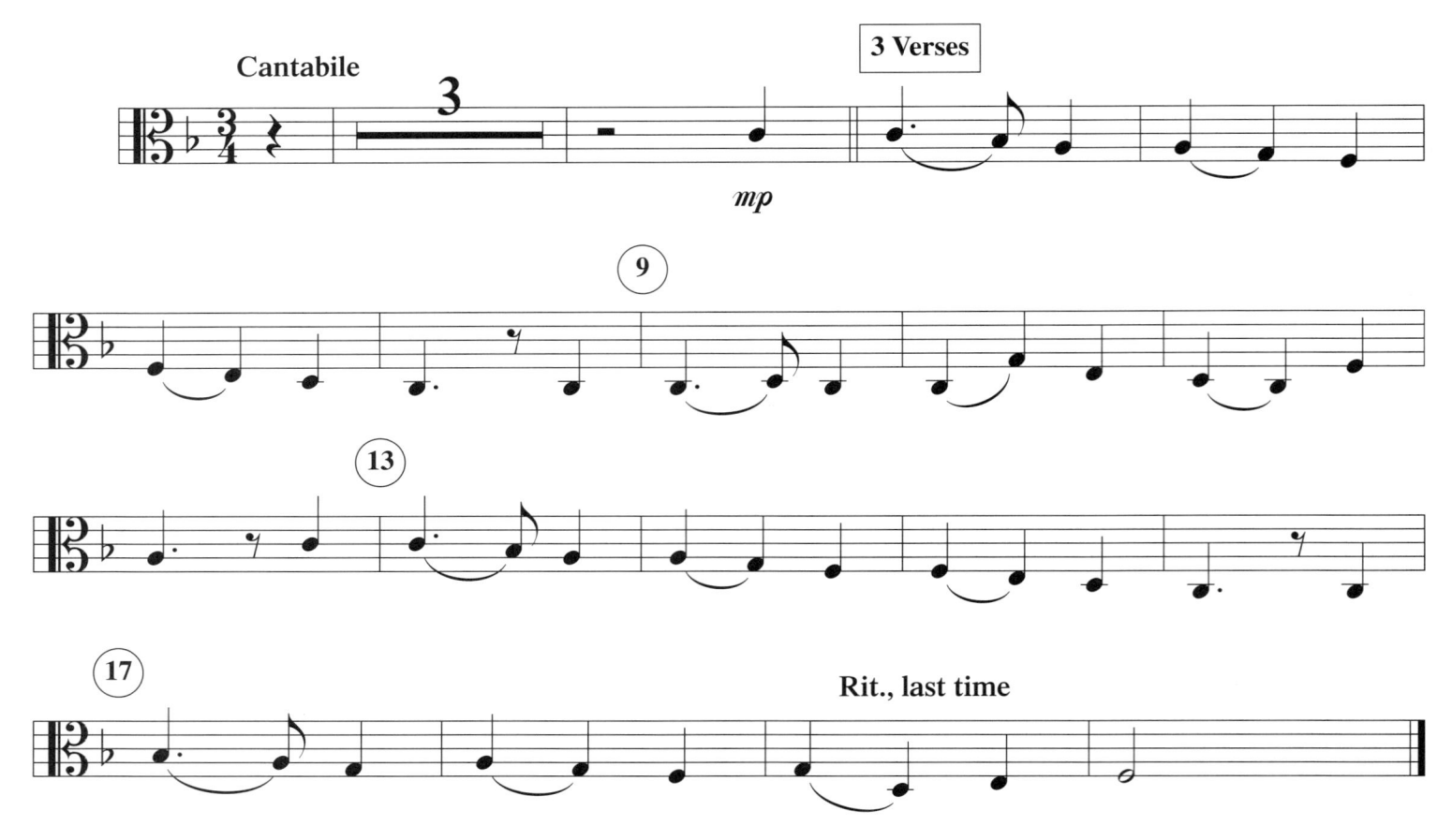

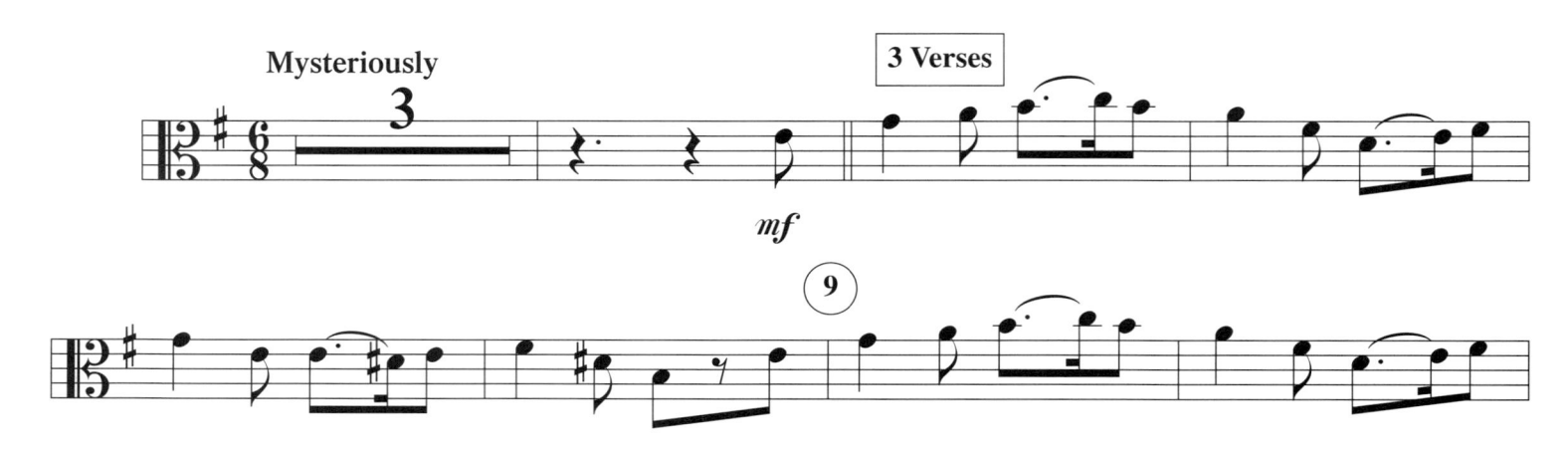

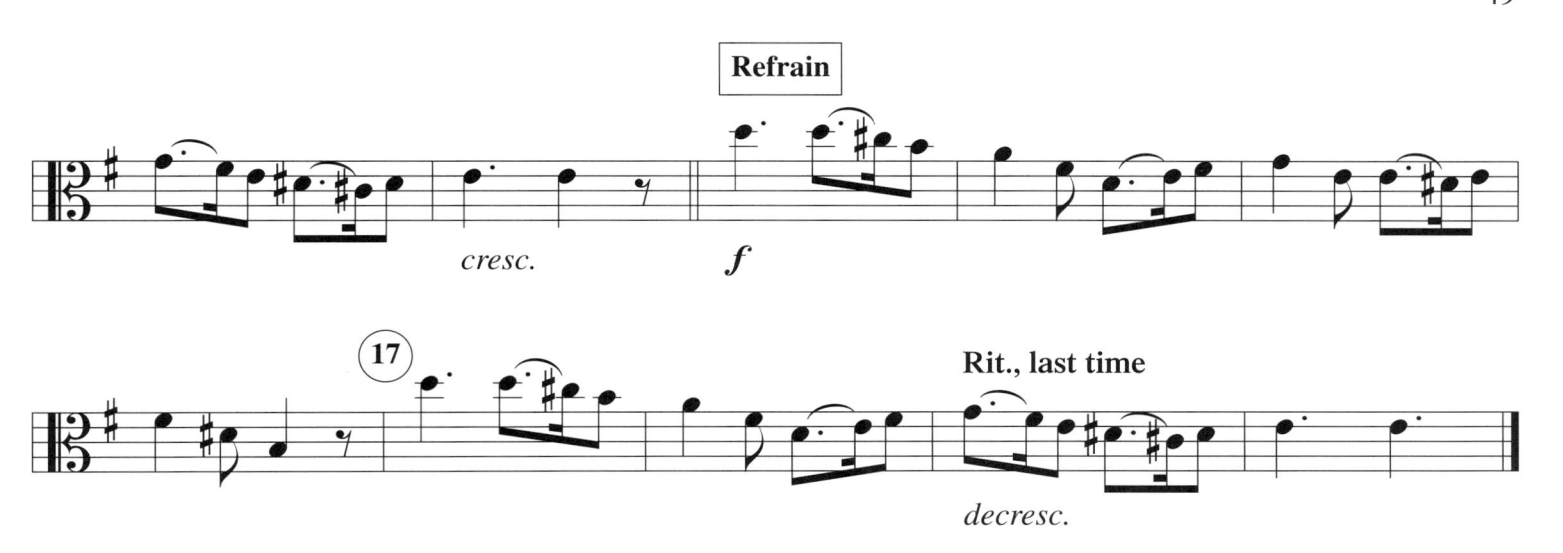

While Shepherds Watched Their Flocks

Alto Clef

GEORGE FREDERICK HANDEL

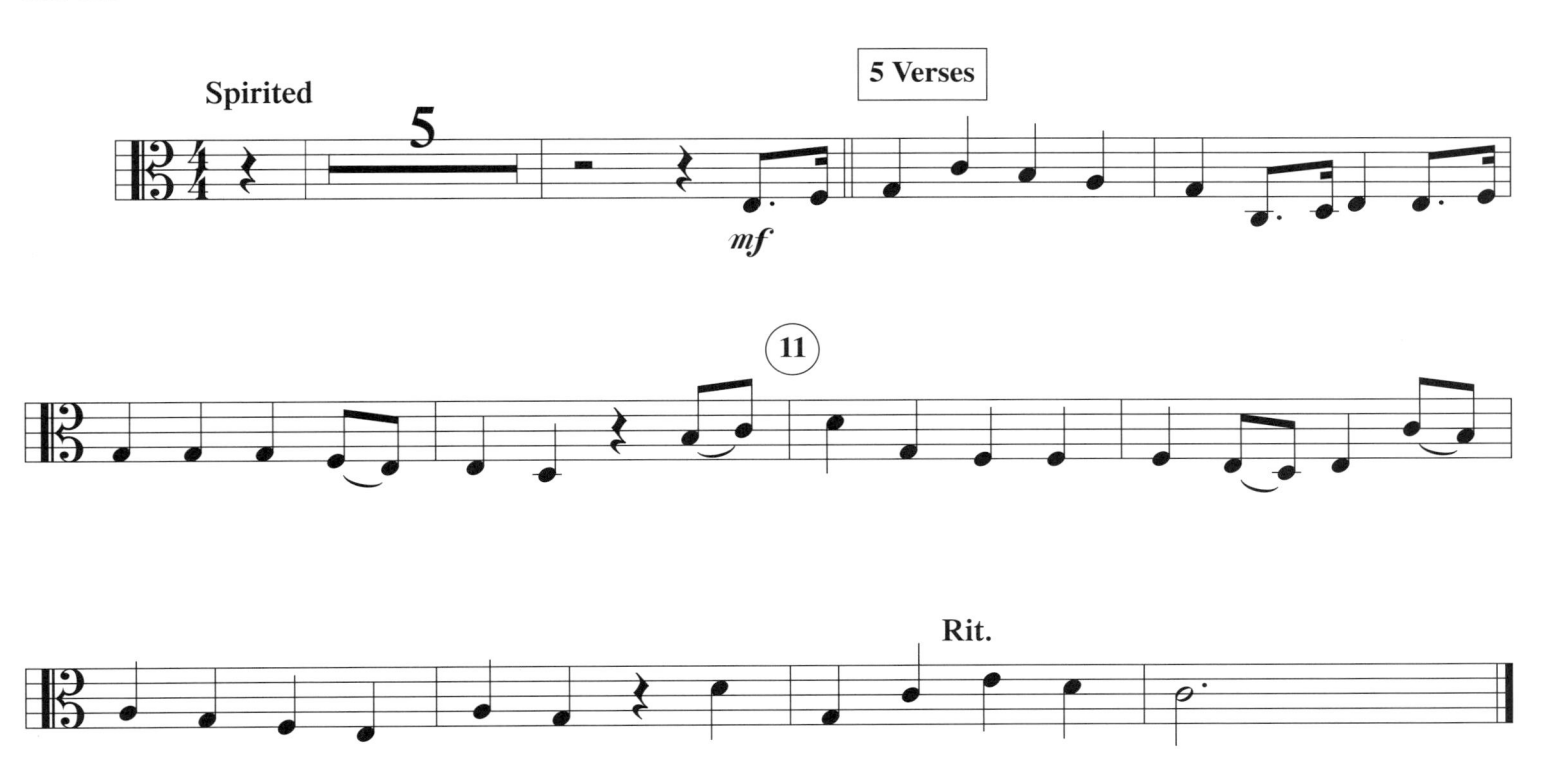

Arr. © 2002 by Lillenas Publishing Company (SESAC). All rights reserved.
Administered by The Copyright Company, 1025 16th Avenue South, Nashville, TN 37212.

HOW TO USE A MIDI FILE

Also available with this solo series on a 3.5" disk called a MIDI file. MIDI files are extremely helpful in education and performance. These MIDI files can be played in most of today's keyboards and on any General MIDI-equipped computer. (A General MIDI sound card is required and MIDI files playback software—included with the sound card.) MIDI is very flexible and will allow you to change the tempo, change the key, repeat sections or delete them, even change the instrumentation of the accompaniment.

On a computer you can load the file onto your hard drive just like any other computer file. Launch you MIDI file payback software, load the song file (MIDI file) you want to play and play the MIDI file. The software will allow you to change the tempo or the key. Some software will even allow you to delete the verse or repeat specific sections. This is extremely helpful when you want to rehearse a specific area of your solo—phrasing, dynamics, or correct notes.

On a General MIDI keyboard (you know it is a General MIDI keyboard by the GM logo printed on the instrument) insert the disk into the disk drive and play the file. Your keyboard manual will have the instructions for all the various adjustments—tempo change, key change, or any edition parameter. We recommend that you save any edits on a disk different from the master file so you can always come back to the original.

MIDI is that simple and that flexible. However, like any technology, practice with it before you perform. Make certain you can hear the file during your performance and the sound technicians have rehearsed with you. Enjoy the richness of these great hymns, and bless the Lord with your instrument.

CONTENTS

C Treble Instruments
- Away in the Manger 8
- It Came upon the Midnight Clear 5
- Joy to the World. 6
- O Come, All Ye Faithful 6
- O Come, O Come, Emmanuel 4
- O Little Town of Bethlehem 4
- Silent Night! Holy Night! 3
- The First Noel 2
- What Child Is This? 8
- While Shepherds Watched Their Flocks. . . . 9

C Bass Instruments
- Away in the Manger 16
- It Came upon the Midnight Clear 13
- Joy to the World. 14
- O Come, All Ye Faithful 14
- O Come, O Come, Emmanuel 12
- O Little Town of Bethlehem 12
- Silent Night! Holy Night! 11
- The First Noel 10
- What Child Is This? 16
- While Shepherds Watched Their Flocks. . . . 17

B♭ Instruments
- Away in the Manger 24
- It Came upon the Midnight Clear 21
- Joy to the World. 22
- O Come, All Ye Faithful 22
- O Come, O Come, Emmanuel 20
- O Little Town of Bethlehem 20
- Silent Night! Holy Night! 19
- The First Noel 18
- What Child Is This? 24
- While Shepherds Watched Their Flocks. . . . 25

F Instruments
- Away in the Manger 32
- It Came upon the Midnight Clear 29
- Joy to the World. 30
- O Come, All Ye Faithful 30
- O Come, O Come, Emmanuel 28
- O Little Town of Bethlehem 28
- Silent Night! Holy Night! 27
- The First Noel 26
- What Child Is This? 32
- While Shepherds Watched Their Flocks. . . . 33

E♭ Instruments
- Away in the Manger 40
- It Came upon the Midnight Clear 37
- Joy to the World. 38
- O Come, All Ye Faithful 38
- O Come, O Come, Emmanuel 36
- O Little Town of Bethlehem 36
- Silent Night! Holy Night! 35
- The First Noel 34
- What Child Is This? 40
- While Shepherds Watched Their Flocks. . . . 41

Alto Clef Instruments
- Away in the Manger 48
- It Came upon the Midnight Clear 45
- Joy to the World. 46
- O Come, All Ye Faithful 46
- O Come, O Come, Emmanuel 44
- O Little Town of Bethlehem 44
- Silent Night! Holy Night! 43
- The First Noel 42
- What Child Is This? 48
- While Shepherds Watched Their Flocks. . . . 49

How to Use a MIDI File 51

Piano (Insert section)
- Away in the Manger 15a
- It Came upon the Midnight Clear 7a
- Joy to the World. 11a
- O Come, All Ye Faithful 12a
- O Come, O Come, Emmanuel 2a
- O Little Town of Bethlehem 8a
- Silent Night! Holy Night! 10a
- The First Noel 4a
- What Child Is This? 16a
- While Shepherds Watched Their Flocks. . . 17a